The London Theatre Guide

Richard Andrews

The London Theatre Guide

Written by Richard Andrews
Photography by Derek Kendall
(additional photography see page 237)
Cover photographs:
(top) by Roger Bamber © Alamy
(bottom) by Metro
(back) by Derek Kendall © English Heritage
Edited by Abigail Willis and Tony Whyte

Seating plans designed by Lesley Gilmour
Book design by Metro

Published in 2007 by
Metro Publications
PO Box 6336
London
N1 6PY

Printed and bound in India

British Library Cataloguing in Publication Data.
A catalogue record for this book is available from the British Library.

ISBN 978-1-902910-28-4

Her Majesty's Theatre

Contents

Overture - The History

Act I - The Theatres

Act II- The Booking

Act III - The Night

Finale - Theatregoers London

Acknowledgments

Thanks go to English Heritage for all the photographs they have provided to use within this book. In particular we want to thank Derek Kendall whose keen eye has created many beautiful photographs and June Warrington and Alyson Rogers for their generosity and patience. We are also grateful to all the theatre staff who have provided information at short notice to make sure that this book is as accurate as possible. Abigail Willis deserves special thanks for her efforts in editing the first edition of this book. I am also greatly indebted to Tony Whyte for his editorial and fact checking work on this new edition.

Whitehall Theatre

Introduction

The aim of this book is to provide a complete guide for anyone visiting a London theatre – and in the year 2006 that was over 12 million theatregoers, spending a record £400 million. On a practical level, this book brings together all the essentials, including seating plans and detailed information on the facilities of the West End theatres, plus box office numbers, as well as tips on how to get cheap (or even free) seats. Those who enjoy the history and stories of London's theatres will also find plenty to interest them. For example, there is the tale of actor William Terris, who was murdered by fellow thespian Richard Archer in 1897 outside the Adelphi, and whose ghost is said to roam the still gas-lit alleyways surrounding the theatre to this day. The idiosyncratic customs and language of the theatre have not been neglected either. Here's your chance to find out why actors are called 'thespians', what 'The Half' is, and why it is unlucky to mention the actual name of 'The Scottish Play'.

I have also included in-depth information about the architecture of West End theatres, from the grand design of Benjamin Wyatt's Theatre Royal Drury Lane, London's oldest, and arguably the world's greatest theatre, to the modern steel and glass of the new Sadler's Wells.

Many of the photographs that accompany the text are provided by English Heritage and wonderfully illustrate the grandeur and architectural details to be found in the Capital's theatres. I hope you enjoy the book as much as I have enjoyed writing it, but above all, I hope that it encourages you to visit London's theatres, and experience the magic of live performance for yourselves.

Richard Andrews

2007

AGATHA C

The Mou

55TH

OVERTURE - THE HISTORY

Theatre Facts

◆ The longest running play is Agatha Christie's *The Mousetrap*, which opened at the Ambassadors on 25th November 1952, transferring to the St Martin's next door on 25th March 1974 where it continues to break records. Although originally some actors were in it for long periods – the record is held by Nancy Seabrook who understudied the role of Mrs Boyle for 16 years (6,240 performances) and appeared 72 times – the cast now changes annually.

◆ The longest running comedy is *No Sex Please We're British*, by Anthony Marriott and Alistair Foot which opened at the Strand on 3rd June 1971, transferring to the Garrick in 1982 and again to the Duchess in 1986 where it ended on 5th September 1987.

◆ The longest running musical is *Les Miserables*, which opened at the Barbican on 8 October 1985, then ran at the Palace Theatre, transferred to the Queen's Theatre and is still running. In 2006 it overtook Andrew Lloyd Webber's *Cats*, which closed at the New London Theatre on its 21st birthday.

◆ The world's first musical is claimed by some to be John Gay's *The Beggar's Opera* produced in 1728 by actor manager John Rich at Lincoln's Inn Fields theatre. It was so successful that it became notorious as "having made Gay rich and Rich gay". Folk tunes of the day were interpolated in the story of a notorious criminal, satirising the corruption of politicians and officials. Gay's next work *Polly* (which continued the story) was banned, becoming the first play to be subject to censorship by the Lord Chamberlain.

The Stage is the world's oldest weekly theatre trade paper having first appeared on 31st January 1880.

◆ Britain's first pantomime was staged by John Rich at Lincoln's Inn Fields in 1716, when he played Harlequin in an adaptation of an Italian comic ballet. He continued to present it each Christmas until 1760. The word pantomime was first used to describe a performance at Drury Lane in 1717.

◆ The first British revue was *Under The Clock,* produced in 1893 by Seymour Hicks and Charles Brookfield.

4

◆ The first public playhouse in Britain was The Theatre, constructed outside the city wall to the north in Shoreditch in 1576, built and managed by the actor James Burbage.

◆ The first British star actor was his son Richard Burbage, the actor manager of the Globe, who created most of the leading roles in Shakespeare's plays.

◆ The first actor to be knighted was Henry Irving in 1895, and the first to receive a peerage was Laurence Olivier in 1970.

The shortest play is Samuel Beckett's Breath (1969) which lasts 30 seconds.

◆ Females did not appear on stage until theatres reopened after the restoration of Charles II in 1660. The first recorded performance by a professional actress was Margaret Hughes as Desdemona in *The Moor Of Venice* on 8th December 1660.

◆ Drury Lane became the first theatre in Britain to be entirely lit by gas on 6th September 1817, although the Lyceum had introduced gas lighting for the stage just one month earlier.

◆ The first use of a curtain coincided with the arrival of the proscenium arch in 1660. Initially the curtain was only raised at the beginning of the performance and lowered at the end. From the 1750s it was also lowered in the interval. The first use of a curtain to denote the end of a scene was pioneered by Henry Irving in *The Corsican Brothers* in 1881.

◆ The Royal Shakespeare Company staged the plays with the longest and shortest titles in the same season at the Aldwych in 1964. *The Persecution And Assassination Of Marat As Performed By The Inmates Of The Asylum Of Charenton Under The Direction Of The Marquis De Sade* by Peter Weiss is known for short as *Marat/Sade*. Even so it is still not as short as Henry Living's *Eh?* (or *US* which they performed in 1966).

◆ The most prolific British playwright is Alan Ayckbourn whose 70th play *If I Were You* premiered in 2006. In 1975 he had five plays running simultaneously in London, *The Norman Conquests* (a trilogy), *Absurd Person Singular* and *Absent Friends*. In 2000 his two plays *House* and *Garden* were performed simultaneously with the same cast in the Lyttelton and Olivier auditoria at the National Theatre.

◆ The actor most associated with a particular role was Richard Goolden as Mole in *Toad Of Toad Hall*, A A Milne's stage version of Kenneth Grahame's *Wind In The Willows*, which was produced regularly each Christmas. He first played it at the Lyric in 1930 and finally at the Old Vic in 1979.

◆ At the Richmond theatre in 1787 a Mr Cubit, the actor playing Hamlet, was taken ill in his dressing room immediately before a performance. There being no understudy, the manager (not wishing to refund the admissions) announced that the company would perform the play omitting the character of Hamlet. Sir Walter Scott, who was in the audience, noted that many of his fellow spectators considered the result to be a great improvement.

Fires

The Theatre Royal Drury Lane is so called because its entrance was originally in Drury Lane. It has been rebuilt three times - twice because it burned down. During the rebuilding the orientation of the theatre was turned through 180 degrees so that the stage now backs on to Drury Lane and the entrance is in Catherine Street. As the third theatre burnt down on 24th February 1809, its then owner, the playwright Sheridan, observed proceedings from a nearby tavern. When asked how he could bear to watch his fortune and livelihood going up in smoke he replied "Tis a great pity if a man may not take a drink at his own fireside".

The Royal Opera House Covent Garden has also been twice destroyed by fire, and in one rebuilding its orientation was turned through 90 degrees. When gas lighting was first introduced at Covent Garden the gas was manufactured and stored in the building. After an explosion on 18th November 1828, the theatre reverted to illumination by oil lamp to allay public fears.

Henry Irving finally left the Lyceum in 1902 because a fire destroyed the warehouse in which he stored the sets and costumes he had amassed during his years as a producer, and he did not have sufficient funds to replace them.

Fires became such frequent occurrences in London theatres, that from 1855 the licensing authority ordered the annual inspection of theatres. This was to ensure "1 - Suitable methods of egress, 2 - Sufficient ventilation, 3 - Available and working extinguishers, 4 - General cleanliness".

John Gielgud directed and starred in The Winter's Tale at the Phoenix Theatre in 1951, during which Hazel Terry accidentally set herself alight and had to be doused by fellow actor (and later playwright) John Whiting. Gielgud remarked "I hear cousin Hazel caught fire. The Terry's have always been combustible."

Carpet Fitter, Theatre Royal Drury Lane

Superstitions

Most superstitions and traditions are shrouded in mystery and have no single explanation of their derivation.

Bad Dress Rehearsal – Wishing an actor a bad dress rehearsal is based on the theory that a good dress rehearsal will lead to over confidence and result in a poor first night performance. When I worked with the director John Dexter, on the afternoon of the first night he insisted on running the whole play scene by scene in reverse order. He said it confused the cast sufficiently to make them really concentrate at the performance. Same idea.

Break A Leg – To directly wish someone 'good luck' on the first night of a play is considered a jinx and so the phrase 'break a leg' is used instead. Americans believe this derives from John Wilkes Booth breaking his leg while trying to escape after assassinating Abraham Lincoln, but I can't see where good luck comes into that. Europeans think that it originated from a Yiddish greeting that was used by German airmen during World War I, being the equivalent of 'happy landings', which sounded like the German for 'neck and leg break'. From there it was translated into English and adopted by British airmen, and then by actors. Neither explanation seems very convincing.

Cats – Many theatres have cats (largely because all theatres have mice). One cat was always an investor in the shows that came into his theatre (the crew helped with the paperwork) and did quite nicely out of it. The Adelphi had two who were called Plug and Socket. It is good luck if a cat appears on stage during rehearsals – but bad luck if it appears during a performance. However this has not been borne out by my experience. The only time I have known it happen during a performance was in *Show Boat*, when either Plug or Socket (I can't remember which) walked across the jetty and then lay down and stretched out on the front deck. The show ran for four years.

Christening A Theatre – When a new theatre opens, an actor should throw a piece of coal from the stage to the highest level of the auditorium, before the first audience arrives, in order to guarantee the building's success.

Entrances – In pantomimes, the Good Fairy always enters from stage right, and the Demon King from stage left. This is presumably derived from a number of superstitions about the left being the sinister side. It is also considered unlucky for a visitor to enter a dressing room left foot first. Anyone who does so must exit backwards and re-enter right foot first.

Falling Down On The First Entrance – If an actor falls down on his first entrance it is considered to be lucky, based on the theory that nothing worse can happen during the rest of the performance.

Inside Out – If an actor puts an item of costume or clothing on inside out it must be worn that way for the rest of the performance or day because to change it brings bad luck.

Knitting On Stage Or In The Wings – Everyone knows it brings bad luck – but no one knows why. I don't think it has anything to do with the French Revolution.

Lay A Baby Face Down – If a doll is used as a baby in a play, it should be placed face down on the prop table, so that evil spirits cannot enter it through the eyes – an idea borrowed from the Japanese Noh theatre tradition.

Leaving Soap In The Dressing Room – Apparently if an actor leaves a bar of soap in the dressing room at the end of a run he will never come back. This sounds like an excuse for frugality to me.

Not Saying The Last Line – There is a theory that you are not supposed to say the last line of a play until the first night, a belief dating back to Elizabethan times, in order not to tempt the Gods, as anything which is finished invites disaster. I have never come across anyone who abided by this. It is more likely to bring a technical disaster if the final sequence hasn't been rehearsed properly.

Peacock Feathers – Peacock feathers should never be used in a fan or costume trimming, or be represented in the set, because the eye of the peacock is thought to be an evil one. The set of *Chu Chin Chow*, the first record breaking musical in 1916, had peacocks painted on panelling in the original set design, but they were replaced by turkeys at the last minute. Make what you will of that.

Putting Shoes On The Dressing Table – I don't know why it is supposed to be unlucky, or more to the point, how to counteract it – so best not do it.

Real Flowers On Stage – It is claimed to be unlucky to have real flowers on stage, because their short life might be reflected in the length of the run of the play. I think it more likely to be a tale put about by producers as an excuse for making one bunch of flowers last an entire run.

The Scottish Play – It is regarded as unlucky to utter the word Macbeth, and so it is always referred to as 'the Scottish play', and the leading characters as 'Mr M' and 'Mrs M'. If mentioned in a dressing room the bad luck can be counteracted by leaving the room, turning round three times anti-clockwise (this represents turning back time) and knocking on the door three times to ask for readmittance. Variations include swearing and spitting. Quoting "angels and ministers of grace defend us" can also help. The play's ill-starred reputation may date from its first performance in 1606 when the boy actor playing Mrs M was taken ill an hour before it started and died before it was completed. There have been productions that have been dogged by bad luck, but these are a reinforcement of the legend rather than its origin. Some people believe that the witches' incantation at the beginning means that it is cursed. Others that it was a victim of its popularity with the public in the 19th century. Whenever a play failed and a guaranteed crowd puller was needed as a substitute, The Scottish Play always fitted the bill. Thus if you mentioned the name it might be needed to do just that.

Spilling Wine The origin is believed to be religious, but exactly why is unknown. The ill fortune is counteracted by putting your finger in it and rubbing it behind your ear.

Thread On A Costume – Someone other than the wearer must take it off, and then the wearer should wind it round his forefinger. The number of revolutions indicates how long the run will be – or alternatively how long until his next contract.

Unlucky Tune – I Dreamt I Dwelt In Marble Halls, a song from the *Bohemian Girl*, is associated with bad luck and should not be whistled, sung or hummed in the theatre in case it invites a similar catastrophe to the show.

Unpacking Make Up Some actors will not unpack their makeup box until after the notices are out, not wanting to presume that they will be in residence very long.

Wearing A Green Costume – One theory why this is believed to be unwise is that limelight had a greenish tinge – combined with a green costume, it would make the actor either invisible or look like a ghost. Another is that the colour was used to represent the devil in medieval mystery plays.

Whistling In The Dressing Room – This is supposed to conjure up an ill wind resulting in a short run. This may have something to do with the fact that stage-hands use whistling as one of the ways in which they communicate and so unnecessary whistling could have unfortunate consequences. It is claimed that the effects of whistling can be counteracted by leaving the room, turning round three times (anti-clockwise) and being invited back in.

Challenging Theatre Superstitions – The Clock Goes Round at the Gielgud Theatre in 1913 challenged superstition by opening on Friday 13th, with thirteen characters, one wearing a green dress and carrying a fan of peacock feathers. Of course superstition was justified as it closed after the thirteenth performance.

Patent Theatres

On 2nd September 1642, during the Civil War, all theatres were closed by parliamentary decree. Following the restoration of Charles II in 1660, Thomas Killigrew and William Davenant were granted a monopoly of theatrical affairs. After some difficulties, in 1662 the King issued them with Patents granting permission to create companies to perform plays. Killigrew formed The Kings Company and built Drury Lane for them to perform in. Davenant established The Duke Of York's Company in a converted tennis court in Lincoln's Inn Fields. His Patent was transferred to Covent Garden in 1732. A third seasonal Patent, which allowed plays to be performed in the summer when the other theatres were closed, was granted to Samuel Foote at the Haymarket in 1766. The Theatres Act of 1843 broke the monopoly of Patent theatres allowing any theatre to perform plays.

Prince Edward Theatre, Dressing Room

Traditions & Terms

The Baddeley Cake – In 1794 an actor called Robert Baddeley, who had played Moses in the first performance of Sheridan's School for Scandal at Drury Lane in 1777, left £100 to be invested to provide a cake and wine for the company playing there every Twelfth Night. With the exception of years during Word War II, the Baddeley cake has been eaten on 6th January each year ever since, and his memory toasted.

Billing – Believe it or not there are more arguments over billing, that is the size and placement of actors names on posters and flyers, than there are over money. It is complicated by there being two prime positions, being billed above any one else, and being billed on the left (as it is the first thing people read). That is why you sometimes see ridiculous compromises where the name on the right is positioned higher than the name on the left.

Burnt Sugar Solution – This is the brown food dye which is diluted to make prop drinks such as whisky, brandy and sherry. Champagne makers Moet & Chandon supply prop champagne in authentic bottles with a lemonade substitute that is quite a pleasant drink.

Call Board – This is the notice board at the stage door where calls (as working sessions are referred to) are posted. These can be rehearsal calls (which may be dance calls or vocal calls), photo calls, band calls - even a rehearsal call for the curtain calls. These notices still observe a traditional formality by referring to people as 'Miss X' and 'Mr Y'. The same formality pertains in announcements: *"Miss Z your call please"*.

Call Boy – Before the days of tannoy systems, a call boy was employed to go round the dressing rooms to call actors to the stage for their entrances. The Haymarket Theatre still employed a call boy until the early 1990s.

Drying – When an actor forgets his/her lines. At which point the stage manager will Prompt by calling out the line. However, this has been known to receive the response: *"We know what the line is but who says it?"*.

Frozen Peas – Most theatres keep a bag of frozen peas to apply as an ice pack to help relieve the pain of injury.

The First Rehearsal – This is when the cast and the creative team all meet for the first time. The set and costume designs are displayed, the script read and the songs sung. It is the ultimate sales pitch. The director sells the script, and the concept of how the show is to be realised, to the cast, and the producer sells the whole package to himself, since he is already committed to spending a significant amount of other people's money. With new work it may be the first time the cast has seen a complete script. The danger signal is when they immediately call their agent at the end of the reading to try to get out of the engagement. I once saw that happen during the coffee break at the interval. There is always a nervous head count of those returning from lunch.

Harlequin – Harlequin wears a costume made up of diamond shapes in colours of great significance: yellow for jealousy, red for love, blue for truth and black for his power of invisibility. He points to a colour to show his mood or his transition to invisibility.

Green Room – The Green Room is a common room where actors can meet, although space is usually at a premium so few theatres actually have them. The first reference to one appears in Thomas Shadwell's play A True Widow in 1678. The name derives from medieval theatre when plays were performed on a grass covered central area around which the audience would gather. 'The Green' has continued as a term for the stage and it is from this that the theatre common room acquires its name.

Has The Ghost Walked? This is a euphemism for "has the manager distributed the pay packets?" It is believed to derive from the fact that actor managers often played the role of the Ghost in Hamlet because it allowed them plenty of free time off stage to deal with the box office returns, make up the wage packets, and pay the cast.

In The Limelight – Limelight was a pre electricity method of lighting, invented by Captain Thomas Drummond in 1816. It was created by playing a high temperature flame onto a piece of lime causing it to glow very brightly. Contained in some sort of housing, the light could be directed at the stage and used to follow the leading actor, making him/her stand out from the others on stage. Although no longer using lime, the basic principle was employed in early film projectors, and was still used in follow spots until fairly recently.

Last Night Practical Jokes – Frustrations built up during a run are often released by playing tricks on fellow artists at the final performance. These take a variety of forms, including tampering with food and drink, gluing shut things which have to be opened, putting stage weights in suitcases, and substituting props - such as replacing cigars in a box with hot dog sausages.

Masks of Comedy and Tragedy – The masks showing smiling or grimacing faces come from the origins of western drama in ancient Greece, when all actors wore masks to denote the sex, age, social standing and mood of the character they were portraying. In recent years opera has been accused of wearing a third mask - Snobbery.

Motivation- When a young actor stopped a rehearsal to ask what his motivation was for a move he was having trouble with, the director John Gielgud replied: "We open tomorrow night."

Pass Door – This is the only connection between the Front Of House - the public part of the theatre - and Backstage - the performers part. Depending on the construction of the building, sometimes this is a very obvious door marked Private just outside the entrance to the stalls or stalls boxes, sometimes it is a concealed door in the wall of stalls itself. Usually you will see the company manager go through it to the stage to start the show once the audience is seated and the auditorium doors have been closed.

Pickfords – In one of the last remaining examples of restrictive industrial practices in Britain, actors who move furniture during scene changes are entitled to receive an extra per performance payment. This is known as Pickfords after the famous removal company.

Show Report – The stage manager's report filled out for each performance, which includes the curtain up and curtain down times (in order to ensure the show's length remains consistent) and any untoward incidents that occurred, such as this genuine example: 'in Act I Scene 1 the door handle came off in his hand so Mr Plinge was forced to exit through the fireplace'.

The Spotlight – The actor's directory used by casting agents, containing their photograph, physical description and agent's contact details.

Surprise Pink – A colour filter that was traditionally known to help to actresses of a certain age to retain/regain their youthful looks. The surprise is that although its real name (Pale Lavender) accurately describes its colour, when artificial light shines through it the result is an enhancing pink.

Thespians – Thespis was a writer, actor and producer in ancient Greece, and the winner of the first ever play competition in 534BC. He is credited with introducing the first solo actor to the theatre, which until then had been conducted entirely by a chorus. Thus the solo actors in his company became known as thespians.

Trap – An opening in the stage floor. A Grave Trap is a rectangle large enough to take a coffin (as used in Hamlet). A Star Trap is circular and made up of triangular sprung leaves opening upwards so that an actor can be propelled through from underneath the stage to magically appear (usually accompanied by a puff of smoke). A Vampire Trap is circular and made up of two sprung leaves opening downwards so that an actor can sink through the stage to magically disappear (usually accompanied by a puff of smoke). It is so named because it was first used in a production of *The Vampire* at the Lyceum in 1820.

Twofer 'Two for the price of one' – A discount voucher. Although this is generally acknowledged to be a New York invention, a Privilege Ticket, granting two seats for the price of one, was introduced at the Aldwych Theatre in the late 1930s. Nowadays BOGOF - as in 'Buy One Get One Free.' - seems to be the rage.

Walter Plinge – The pseudonym used for disguise purposes in billing and programmes. For instance, if the producer doesn't want the audience to know that one actor plays two parts or wants to give the impression that there are more actors in the play than there really are. In the US the name Alan Smithee is use for the same purpose.

Ghosts

Adelphi
The actor William Terriss was murdered outside the Royal Entrance in Maiden Lane (where the stage door is now) by rival actor Richard Archer Prince in 1897. He is said to haunt Bullen Court, the alley that runs alongside the theatre linking the Strand and Maiden Lane (where the stage door was then) wearing a frock coat and top hat

Duke Of York's
An iron fire door that was removed many decades ago is heard to slam every night at ten o'clock. Some years ago an old fashioned key with a tag marked Iron Door dropped at the feet of the manager.

A female figure dressed in black has been seen wandering through the circle bar. It is said to be the ghost of Violet Melnotte the original owner, known to everyone as 'Madame'.

'The Strangler Jacket', a costume said to have been purchased from a market stall, became progressively tighter, despite being let out several times. The actress who wore the jacket in a show there in the 1920s suffered feelings of constriction and suffocation

Drury Lane
The Man In Grey, a gentleman in 18th century riding cloak, boots, sword and tricorn hat, walks through one wall at the end of row D, across the upper circle, and disappears into the wall on the other side. The appearance usually occurs during matinees and is considered a sign of good fortune. He is thought to be connected with a skeleton found with a dagger in his ribs bricked up in the wall through which he disappears.

Another ghost, believed to be that of the clown Grimaldi, who gave his farewell appearance at the theatre in 1828, is said to give a guiding hand to actors if they are giving bad performances.

The reflection of comedian and comic actor Dan Leno has been seen in the mirror of his favourite dressing room.

Actor manager Charles Macklin fatally stabbed a fellow actor called Hallam in the eye with a stick in an argument over a wig in the Green Room in 1735. Macklin was convicted of manslaughter but avoided imprisonment by paying a fine to Hallam's family. He stalks the area that used to be the pit.

Garrick
Actors descending a staircase from the dressing rooms to the stage (known as the Phantom Staircase) have reported feeling a slap on the back as an act of encouragement from the presence of former actor manager Arthur Bourchier.

There is also a phantom prompter who whispers lines from the old prompt corner.

Haymarket
John Buckstone, the 19th century actor manager, is said to have loved the theatre so much that he can't bear to leave it. He has been seen many times in the star dressing room, entering through a bricked up former doorway, and also on stage during performances. Because of his great success as a manager this is considered to be a good omen.

Her Majesty's
The actor manager Herbert Beerbohm Tree, who built the current theatre, has been observed making his way from the Dome rooms, where he kept an apartment, to his favourite box.

London Coliseum
A lady in black, believed to be the ghost of a former housekeeper, has been seen in the balcony, and a First World War Subaltern, who visited the theatre on leave before going overseas where he subsequently perished, has been seen in the second row of the upper circle.

London Palladium
A lady in a crinoline has been seen on the old crimson staircase at the rear of the royal circle.

Lyceum
A woman in Civil War period dress has been seen seated in the stalls, holding the severed head of a man. She is believed to be the ghost of an ancestor of the Courtney family, owners of the original building, whose husband was beheaded by Oliver Cromwell.

Lyric
The front of house area is reputedly haunted by the ghost of Nellie Klute, a murdered programme seller.

Noel Coward
A distinguished Victorian gentleman with wavy grey hair, believed to be the ghost of Charles Wyndham, the actor manager who built the theatre, has been seen backstage.

Old Vic
A woman clasping her bloodstained hands to her breast has been seen backstage, supposedly an actress playing Mrs M in 'the Scottish play', who, not wanting to take her final bow, repeats the sleepwalking scene over and over again.

Palace
The ballet dancer Anna Pavlova made her London debut there in 1910, and her ghost has been seen in various parts of the building.

Peacock
There have been sightings of the ghost of an unknown actress, reputedly the mistress of Oscar Hammerstein, who built the original theatre on this site in 1911.

Sadler's Wells
The head of Joseph Grimaldi, (severed from his body before burial at his own request) was seen in full clown make up, watching the show over the shoulders of the occupants of one of the boxes in the old theatre. Grimaldi made his debut there at the age of three.

St George's Hall
John Neville Maskelyne, one of the famous conjuring and magic family, has been spotted on stage performing the plate spinning act which made him famous.

Theatre Architects

Bertie Crewe (d 1937)

Lyceum (interior), Phoenix (with Sir Giles Gilbert Scott and Cecil Masey), Piccadilly (with Edward A Stone), Royal Court (with Walter Emden), Shaftesbury

Apprenticed to Clement Dowling and Frank Matcham in London, Bertie Crewe also spent some time with Atelier Laloux in Paris working on buildings such as the Gare D'Orsay. He specialised entirely in theatres, and later cinemas. After a period of relatively restrained work with C J Phipps, he developed a flamboyant style with Baroque touches and a delight in elaborate, even extravagant decoration that was completely three dimensional. Crewe was particularly skilled in creating impressive façades that matched the theatricality of their interiors. With the Stoll theatre, probably his greatest work, he created a magnificent opera house in the continental fashion.

Apollo Victoria

Walter Emden (1847-1913)
Duke of York's, Garrick (with C J Phipps), Royal Court (with Bertie Crewe)

The son of a theatre proprietor Walter Emden began as a scenic designer, before studying civil engineering and finally architecture at Kelly and Lawes. Probably betraying his lack of formal training, Emden's early work displayed a vast range of styles. Terry's theatre looked like a public house, while the Tivoli had the appearance of a palace of varieties. His later work was more restrained, with the Duke of York's looking like a grand private house, and the Garrick boasting a classically inspired colonnade. Emden also designed many restaurants, hotels and other places of entertainment

Frank Matcham (1854-1920)
Coliseum, London Palladium, Victoria Palace. Also Hackney Empire, Richmond Theatre.

Frank Matcham was the most prolific and innovative theatre architect the world has known. He was born in Newton Abbot, the son of a brewery manager, and was apprenticed to George S Bridgeman, a local architect, where he discovered his love for theatre architecture. Matcham went to work in the practice of Jethro T Robinson, who was Consulting Theatre Architect to the Lord Chamberlain, and in 1877 married Robinson's daughter Maria. Robinson's unexpected death the following year opened the way for Matcham to take over one of the most prestigious architectural practices in London at the age of 24. His work rate was prodigious, and by 1880 he had become the most sought after theatre architect in the country specialising in the larger and more extravagant music halls, lyric theatres and opera houses. Only nine of his thirty theatres survive, but they illustrate his talent for handsome decoration and excellent sightlines. Matcham's greatest technical innovation was in pioneering the use of the cantilevered auditorium, thus eliminating the need for pillars to support the circles.

C J Phipps (1835-1897)
Garrick (with Walter Emden), Her Majesty's, Lyric, Vaudeville (exterior)

Born in Bath, Charles John Phipps was articled to local architects Wilcox and Fuller, before starting his own practice, and then moving to London in 1863. He was a prolific designer of theatres, hotels, apartment blocks and public buildings. Phipps specialised in play houses rather than lyric theatres or music halls, which are characterised by restraint and low relief decoration in contrast to the flamboyance of Matcham or Crewe. His early work lent towards the Gothic and ecclesiastical, but he later adopted a more classical style. His exteriors exude a solid civic dignity; Her Majesty's, showing his partiality for French theatrical design, could almost be an Hotel de Ville.

W G R Sprague (1863-1933)
Albery, Aldwych, Gielgud, Ambassadors, Queen's, St Martin's, Strand, Wyndhams

Sprague was born in Australia to an English actress Dolores Drummond, who returned to England in 1874. At 16 he was apprenticed to Matcham for four years, and then to Emden for a further three before setting up on his own. Continued study ensured that he was probably the best trained architect of the period with great breadth of technical and stylistic knowledge. Unlike many others, he ensured that his exteriors were at one with his interiors. Sprague specialised in intimate and elegant play houses, influenced by 19th century French style, but in his own distinctive manner. His particular forte was twin theatres with subtle variations.

Edward A Stone
Piccadilly (with Bertie Crewe), Prince Edward, Whitehall

Edward Stone was one of the most successful designers of cinemas and cine-theatres, some of which had impressive provision for stage shows. He was of a later generation than the other major architects, producing Art Deco influenced buildings. It was frequently his practice to entrust the interiors of his theatres to specialists. Stone's work also included the Astorias at Brixton (now Academy) and Finsbury Park (later the Rainbow) whose 'atmospheric' design schemes featured lavishly detailed Mediterranean and Arabian townscapes surrounding the prosceniums and decorating the side walls of the auditoria, and night sky ceilings with twinkling stars.

Thomas Verity (1837-1891)
Comedy, Criterion

Thomas Verity was articled to an architect employed by the War Office, working on the South Kensington Museum, and was principal assistant on the design of the Royal Albert Hall 1867-70. He won a competition to design the Criterion restaurant and concert hall that later became a theatre. From 1870 to his death he was Consulting Theatre Architect to the Lord Chamberlain. A great Francophile, his theatres show the influence of French Second Empire and later the Beaux-Arts tradition. The interior scheme of decorated ceramic tiles and mirrors of the Criterion is unique. Verity also designed many non-theatrical buildings.

First Nights - 'Darling you were wonderful!'

The most famous overheard comment from someone leaving the theatre after witnessing the first night of Sarah Bernhard's histrionic performance as Cleopatra in Antony And Cleopatra: *"How very unlike the home life of our own dear Queen"*.

Two people leaving the Old Vic on the first night of the disastrous production of Macbeth with Peter O'Toole: *"Well, all I hope now dear is that the dog has not been sick in the car."*

W S Gilbert is generally credited with the immortal line *"My dear fellow! Good isn't the word!"*

Another school claims it for Oscar Wilde, talking to Herbert Beerbohm Tree on his performance as Hamlet in 1892. But then on a different occasion when Wilde exclaimed *"I wish I'd said that"* he received the repost *"You will Oscar, you will"*.

Henry Irving's comment to American actor Richard Mansfield when he complained about the strain of playing both Dr Jekyll and Mr Hyde was *"if it's unendurable, why do it?"*

It was W S Gilbert who after witnessing Arthur Bourchier's Hamlet said: *"at last we can settle whether Bacon or Shakespeare wrote the plays. Have both the coffins opened and whoever has turned in his grave is the author."*

Ned Sherrin entered a distinguished actress's dressing room with *"You were wonderful - but you can take off that dreadful false nose now"* only to receive the response *"I already have"*.

The best line I have heard personally is *"You did it again!"* which of course could mean absolutely anything. You can also hedge your bets with *"Well, how about you?"* along with *"Well, what can I say!"*.

When people are at a loss for words, they usually take refuge in being overly enthusiastic about the scenery and costumes, but the nadir is believed to have been the person who ventured *"The brass-work in the stalls was beautifully polished"*.

Theatre Information Key

♿	Wheelchair Access
▲	Steps Up to Level
▼	Steps Down to Level
👥	Seating Capacity
◉	Special Feature

Duchess Theatre

ACT I - THE THEATRES

Theatre Information

History, location, facilities, and seating plan
for each of the West End theatres

Other Venues

Adelphi

The Strand WC2R 0NS
Box office: 0870 8955598
Website: www.rutheatres.com
Tube: Charing Cross/Covent Garden/Leicester Square
Train: Charing Cross
Parking: Bedfordbury/Trafalgar Square
✳ Air Condition   ◁ Infra-red
⊙ *Stalls bars contain displays of memorabilia relating to Vivian Ellis and Jessie Matthews.*

There have been theatres on this site since 1806 when John Scott built the Sans Pareil for his daughter to perform in, opening with *Miss Scott's Entertainments*. It was renamed the Adelphi after its 1819 refurbishment, when it became one of the first London theatres to be lit by a gas chandelier. In 1834 the first mechanical sinking stage in Britain was installed. Popular theatre, musicals or light entertainment, have been its staple. The original license was for the presentation of 'burlettas' – dramas that included at least five pieces of vocal music in each act. As a result even Othello had piano accompaniment when it was presented here. The present building, designed by Ernest Schaufelberg in 1930, is notable for its Art Deco style and the complete absence of curves in its construction. Straight lines and angles dominate the theatre's decorative scheme both inside and out. The exterior is remarkable for its large irregular octagon window at first floor level, restored in 1993, and the foyer for its black marble walls and chrome fittings. Dramatic versions of Dickens novels were presented here almost as soon as they appeared in print, including *Nicholas Nickleby*, *Oliver Twist* and *A Christmas Carol* (1837-45). In 1897 the actor William Terriss was murdered by a jealous rival as he was entering the theatre by the Royal Entrance in Maiden Lane. The early years of the twentieth century saw a succession of operettas and musicals including *The Quaker Girl* (1910), Gladys Cooper in *Peter Pan* (1923), Evelyn Laye in *Betty In Mayfair* (1925), and Vivian Ellis's *Mr Cinders* (1929). Under the management of Charles B Cochran it became a home for revue with Jessie Matthews in *Evergreen* (1930) and Noel Coward's *Words And Music* (1932). Cole Porter's *Nymph Errant* (1933), Ivor Novello's *The Dancing Years* (1942), and *Bless The Bride* (1947) followed. Musicals returned with Lionel Bart's *Blitz!* (1962) which became famous as the show where "people came out humming the scenery" and *Maggie May* (1964), Anna Neagle in *Charlie Girl* (1965), *Show Boat* (1971), Stephen Sondheim's *A Little Night Music* (1975) and *Me And My Girl* (1985). Recently there has been Andrew Lloyd Webber's *Sunset Boulevard* (1993), an 8 year run of *Chicago* (1997) and a new production of *Joseph and the Amazing Technicolour Dreamcoat* (2007).

ADELPHI

Upper Circle

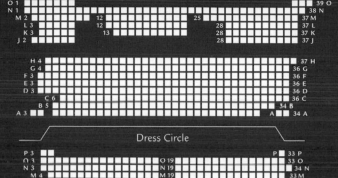

O 1 — 39 O
N 1 — 38 N
M 2 — 12 — 25 — 37 M
L 3 — 12 — 28 — 37 L
K 3 — 13 — 28 — 37 K
J 2 — 28 — 37 J

H 4 — 37 H
G 4 — 36 G
F 3 — 36 F
E 3 — 36 E
D 3 — 36 D
C 6 — 36 C
B 5 — 34 B
A 3 — A — 34 A

Dress Circle

P 3 — P 33 P
O 3 — O 19 — 33 O
N 3 — N 19 — 34 N
M 4 — M 19 — 33 M
L 3 — L 19 — 34 L
K 4 — K 19 — 33 K
J 4 — J 19 — 34 J
H 4 — H 19 — 33 H
G 3 — G 19 — 34 G
F 4 — F 19 — 33 F
E 3 — E 19 — 34 E
D 4 — D 19 — 33 D
C 4 — 35 C
B 5 — 34 B
A 6 — A — 33 A

Stalls

X 6 — X 23 — 33 X
W 4 — W 19 — 33 W
V 4 — V 19 — 33 V
U 3 — U 19 — 33 U
T 1 — T 19 — 32 T
S 4 — S 19 — 32 S
R 4 — R 19 — 32 R
P 4 — P 19 — 33 P
O 4 — O 19 — 33 O
N 4 — N 19 — 33 N
M 4 — M 19 — 33 M
L 4 — L 19 — 33 L
K 5 — K 19 — 33 K
J 3 — 34 J
H 3 — 34 H
G 4 — 34 G
F 3 — 33 F
E 4 — 33 E
D 4 — 32 D
C 6 — 32 C
B 6 — 31 B
A 7 — 30 A
BB 10 — 26 BB
AA 12 — 23 AA

Box C (left) **Box B** (right)
Box D (left) **Box A** (right)

Stage

▲ 79 Upper Circle ▲ 41 Dress Circle ▲ 0 Stalls ▲ 1 Foyer
🎭 1478

29

Aldwych

The Aldwych, WC2B 4DF
Box office: 0870 400 0805
www.aldwychtheatre.com
Tube: Covent Garden/Holborn/Temple
Train: Charing Cross
Parking: Drury Lane/Bedfordbury Street
✻ Air Condition
♿ Dress Circle
◉ *Foyer shares a two storey high ceiling and chandelier with the Dress Circle bar similar to the Gielgud.*

The Aldwych was designed by W G R Sprague as a twin to the Strand theatre (now the Novello) Both were built in 1905 when the new street The Aldwych was being laid out and 'book-ended' the block accompanied by the Waldorf hotel. The Aldwych has a classical façade in Portland stone with pediments and columns while its interior combines Georgian and French Baroque. The decorative scheme of grey-blue with gilt ornamentation suffered during the "paint it black" era of the Royal Shakespeare Company but has since been restored. Although musical comedies with Seymour Hicks and Ellaline Terriss (whose actor father was murdered outside the Adelphi, see page 28) were a feature of the Aldwych's early years, it was a series of farces which really put the theatre on the map. The Aldwych Farces, as they became known, were written by Ben Travers and included legendary plays such as *A Cookoo In The Nest* (1925), *Rookery Nook* (1926), *Dirty Work* (1932) and *A Bit Of A Test* (1933). The Aldwych enjoyed a second, very different golden age between 1960 and 1982 when it became the London home of the Royal Shakespeare Company. Many Shakespeare productions transferred here from Stratford during the directorships of Peter Hall and Trevor Nunn, including the eight play history cycle, *The Wars Of The Roses* (1965), and Peter Brook's *A Midsummer Night's Dream* (1971). These alternated with a modern drama repertory that included *Marat/Sade*, Jules Feifer's *Little Murders*, and *US*. Another landmark production was *Nicholas Nickleby* (1979). Every summer between 1964-1973 the Aldwych played host to some of the world's greatest theatres companies, courtesy of Peter Daubney's World Theatre Seasons. The Aldwych saw the British premiers of Chekhov's *The Cherry Orchard* (1911), Tennessee Williams's *A Streetcar Named Desire* (1949) with Vivien Leigh, Anouilh's *Beckett* (1961) and Harold Pinter's *The Homecoming* (1965). In recent years a number of productions have transferred here from the National Theatre, among them Jim Cartwright's *The Rise And Fall Of Little Voice* (1992), J B Priestley's *An Inspector Calls* (1993) and David Hare's *Amy's View* (1998) with Judi Dench. One of its longest runners was the musical *Fame* (2002). Currently showing is the hugely popular *Dirty Dancing*.

ALDWYCH

Upper Circle

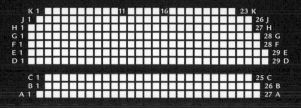

Dress Circle

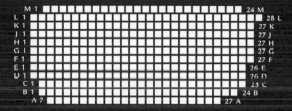

Stalls

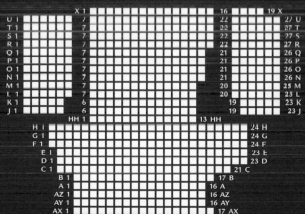

Stage

▲ 24 Upper Circle ▲ 15 Dress Circle ▼ 26 Stalls ▲ 6 Foyer
🏛 1200

Ambassadors

West Street WC2H 9ND
Box office: 0870 060 6627
Website: www.newambassadors.com
Tube: Leicester Square/Covent Garden
Train: Charing Cross
Parking: Upper St Martin's Lane/Shelton Street
✻ *Air Condition*
◉ *A sculpture next to the box office marks the run of The Mousetrap.*

Conceived as a pair with the St Martin's next door, and designed by twin-
ning expert W G R Sprague, the Ambassadors opened in 1913. The site is
very restricted in all directions and the building is a great feat of compres-
sion. Legend has it that it was about to open when it was realised that
there was no box office, and because the foyer was too small to build one,
the ladies toilet had to be converted to fill the bill – although this seems an
unlikely oversight for someone like Sprague. It has a simple classical façade
in red brick and stucco. The auditorium is a miniature version of Sprague's
other theatres, an intimate elegant Louis XVI style, decorated with ambas-
sadorial crests. These were painted out at the outbreak of hostilities in
1914 and only restored in 1958. C B Cochran introduced intimate revue
to London here with Alice Delysia in *Odds And Ends* (1914), *More (Odds
And Ends)* (1915) and *Pell Mell* (1916). A succession of quality plays introduced new performers to London audiences including Ivor Novello in
Debrau (1921) Hermione Gingold in *If* (1921), Paul Robeson in *The Emperor Jones* (1925), Margaret Lockwood in *Family Affairs* (1934) and Vivien
Leigh in *The Mask Of Virtues* (1935). Revue returned in World War II
with *The Gate Revue* (1939), *Swinging At The Gate* (1940), *Sweet And Low*
(1943), *Sweeter And Lower* (1944) and *Sweetest And Lowest* (1946) all starring
Hermione Gingold. Its place in history was assured when Agatha Christie's *The Mousetrap* (1952) opened, although it transferred to the larger St
Martin's (an unheard of step) in 1974. The longest runner since then was
the Royal Shakespeare Company production of Christopher Hampton's
adaptation of *Les Liaisons Dangerouses* (1986), with Lindsay Duncan and
Alan Rickman. The Royal Court moved its Theatre Upstairs productions
here while its Sloane Square home was refurbished from 1996 to 1999,
dividing the building to create two spaces, using the circle and the stage
as separate playing areas. In 1999 it was relaunched as the Ambassadors,
presenting limited runs of new writing or classic revivals by touring companies, since when productions have included *Stones In His Pockets* (2000)
The Bomb-Itty Of Errors (2003) and *Sweeney Todd* (2004).

AMBASSADORS

Circle

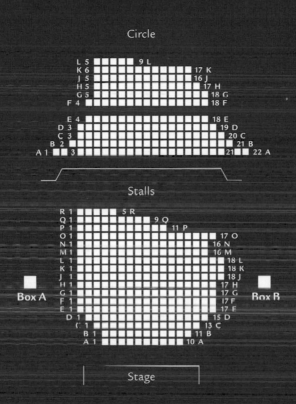

Stalls

Box A

Box B

Stage

5 ▲ *Dress Circle, 26 ▼ Stalls, 1 ▲ Foyer,* 🏛 *418*

Apollo

Shaftesbury Avenue, W1V 7DH
Box office: 0870 890 1101
www.nimaxtheatres.com
Tube: Piccadilly Circus
Train: Charing Cross
Parking: Brewer Street/Denman Street
✳ Air Condition   ◀ Infra-red
⊙ To the right of the entrance there is the coat of arms, a silver chain and buckle with a flying lizard supported by two lions rampant.

The only theatre designed by Lewin Sharp, the Apollo was envisaged as a home for musical entertainments, with an orchestra pit inspired by the opera house at Bayreuth, and much care given to the acoustics. In fact, ever since it opened in 1901, it has mostly housed light comedies, with musicals going to the slightly larger Lyric next door. Architecturally it is strikingly different from the other Shaftesbury Avenue theatres, with a façade in French renaissance style, and winged figures adorning the domed towers which make up its top story. The coat of arms at the entrance is the badge of a group of gypsies with whom Henry Lowenfield, the original owner, was connected. This device was supposed to bring good luck and formed a major part of the original design scheme for the building, which at one stage was to have been called the Mascot. The auditorium, which is notable for its lack of pillars, is decorated in an opulent Louis XIV style, with statuary supporting the boxes. The first big success here was H G Pelissier's *The Follies* (1908-1912) which laid the foundations for intimate revue. Later revues were Jack Hulbert and Cicely Courtneidge in *By The Way* (1925), *For Amusement Only* (1956), and *Pieces Of Eight* (1959) with Kenneth Williams and Fenella Fielding. Marion Lorne starred in a series of plays written and produced for her by her husband Walter Hackett, including *Hyde Park Corner* (1934), and *London After Dark* (1937). Among the premieres it has seen are Harold Brighouse's *Hobson's Choice* (1916), Terence Rattigan's *Flare Path* (1942), *The Happiest Days Of Your Life* (1948) with Margaret Rutherford, Alan Bennett's *Forty Years On* (1968) and Keith Waterhouse's *Jeffrey Bernard Is Unwell* (1989) with Peter O'Toole. Other notable productions include *Abie's Irish Rose* (1927), Sean O'Casey's *The Silver Tassie* (1929), Robert Sherwood's *Idiot's Delight* (1938) with Raymond Massey, and *Seagulls Over Sorrento* (1950). The Apollo's longest run was provided by Marc Camoletti's *Boeing-Boeing* (1962), which transferred after 3 years. More recently it has been home to another Camoletti farce, *Don't Dress For Dinner* (1991), Felicity Kendal and Frances De La Tour in *Fallen Angel* (2000) and Warren Mitchell in *The Price* (2003).

APOLLO

Balcony

Upper Circle

Dress Circle

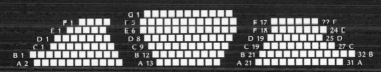

Stalls

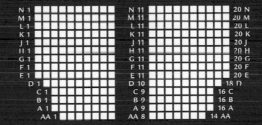

Stage

▲ 60 Balcony ▼ 40 Upper Circle ▼ 12 Dress Circle ▼ 2 Stalls ▲ 1 Foyer
775

Apollo Victoria
Wilton Road SW1V 1LL
Box office: 0870 4000 8000
Website: www.livenation.co.uk
Tube: Victoria
Train: Victoria
Parking: Rochester Row/Vauxhall Bridge Road
♿ *Dress Circle*
✶ *Air Condition*   ♤ *Infra-red*
◉ *Fine Art Deco architectural details.*

The Apollo Victoria was originally built as a super cinema and opened in 1930, as the New Victoria Cinema. One of the most architecturally important cinemas in Britain, it was the first to be built in the Germanic expressionist style. Its scale is grand, originally accommodating 2,500 people, with the stalls seating extending out under the pavements. The foyer spans the entire block with two entrances, one in Wilton Road and the other in Vauxhall Bridge Road. It was designed by E Warmsley Lewis with a modern marble and concrete exterior, which is ribbed like a gigantic radio set, and includes reliefs of cinemagoers by W E Trent on either side of the Wilton Road entrance. The interior has an underwater theme, with fish, shells and sea flora motifs while the circle was designed like an ocean liner with portholes in the doors. Most of the sculpture and decorative work is by Trent and much of it remains today, including a bronze reclining mermaid in Cleopatra style above the entrance to the Gents, and a nude in the foyer juggling with reels of film. The venue was conceived as a cine-variety house and opened with a programme that comprised *Hoop-La*, a stage show, Reginald Foort at the organ, and the film *Old England*. Stage shows were soon dropped, but appearances by big bands and live acts continued throughout the 1930s. George V attended a Royal Charity matinée of *The Good Companions* here in 1933. Theatrical use began after its facilities were upgraded in 1958, with ad hoc concerts and later appearances by London Festival Ballet, as large cinemas went out of fashion. In 1972 it was the first cinema to achieve Listed Building status. It closed in 1975 and was relaunched as Apollo Victoria in 1981, with moderately successful revivals of *The Sound Of Music* (1981) *Camelot* (1982) and *Fiddler On The Roof* (1983). The auditorium was subsequently reconfigured, losing 1000 seats in the process, to accommodate the skating rink for *Starlight Express* (1984). This also resulted in some of the decorative features being removed, repainted or obscured. Following the closure of *Starlight Express* in January 2002, the auditorium has been sympathetically restored to its pre 1984 grandeur with many of the architectural features being uncovered and repaired. In 2006 the Art Deco features of the foyer were fully restored as part of the programme.

Apollo Victoria

APOLLO VICTORIA

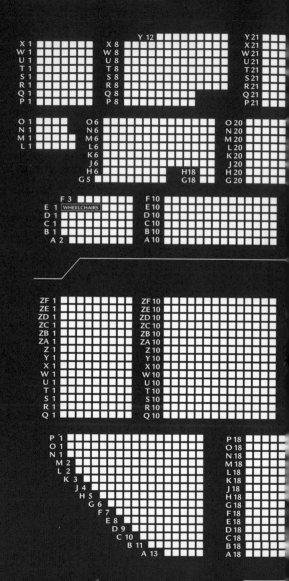

Y 31
X 31
W 31
U 31
T 31
S 31
R 31
Q 35
P 35

X 44   50 X
W 44   50 W
U 44   50 U
T 44   50 T
S 44   50 S
R 44   50 R
Q 44   50 Q
P 44   50 P

O 34   O 49   52 O
N 34   N 49   52 N
M 34   M 48   52 M
L 34   L 48   52 L
K 34
J 34
H 34   H 40
G 34   G 40

F 24   F 36   44 F
E 24   E 38   E
D 24   D 38   46 D
C 24   C 38   46 C
B 24   B 38   46 B
A 24   A 38   45 A

WHEELCHAIRS

ZF 24   ZF 38   46 ZF
ZE 24   ZE 38   46 ZE
ZD 24   ZD 38   46 ZD
ZC 24   ZC 38   46 ZC
ZB 24   ZB 38   46 ZB
ZA 24   ZA 38   46 ZA
Z 24   Z 38   46 Z
Y 24   Y 38   46 Y
X 24   X 38   46 X
W 24   W 38   46 W
U 24   U 38   46 U
T 24   T 38   46 T
S 24   S 38   46 S
R 24   R 38   46 R
Q 24   Q 38   46 Q

P 32   48 P
O 32   48 O
N 32   48 N
M 32   47 M
L 32   47 L
K 32   46 K
J 32   45 J
H 32   44 H
G 32   43 G
F 32   42 F
E 32   41 E
D 32   40 D
C 32   39 C
B 32   38 B
A 32   36 A

▲ 13 Dress Circle ▼ 29 Stalls ▲ 4 Wilton Road Foyer,
▲ 9 Vauxhall Bridge Foyer ♿1524+40 standing

39

Barbican

Silk Street, EC2Y 8BQ
Box office: 020 7638 8891
Website: www.barbican.org.uk
Tube: Moorgate/Barbican
Train: Moorgate/Farringdon
Parking: Beneath the theatre

✻ Air Condition   ◁ Infra-red

⊙ *Waterside restaurant, bookshop, pre-show entertainment, foyer open all day, conservatory and sculpture court on the roof*

In 1959 the Corporation of the City of London agreed a scheme for a residential development with a theatre and concert hall for the Guildhall School of Music and Drama in an area that had been destroyed by bombing in World War II. In 1962 it was decided that the theatre and concert hall should be reserved for professional companies, and in 1964 the Royal Shakespeare Company and the London Symphony Orchestra became the designated companies, involved in the design. The residential development went ahead, but it took eighteen years and numerous changes of personnel, minds, and plans, alarming budgetary rises, near cancellations and conceptual revisions before it opened in 1982. By this time the planning vogue of the 1960s with its wholesale redevelopment of areas, eliminating street patterns and separating pedestrians from traffic with walkways had been discredited, but here was a scheme which did just that. It became a standing joke that no-one could find their way into the building, and when they did, they couldn't find the level of the theatre or concert hall they wanted. Various facelifts, signage schemes, renumbering of levels and internal bridges have been tried by successive managerial regimes, but the struggle continues. In addition to the theatre and concert hall the centre finally included the Pit studio theatre, 3 cinemas, exhibition and conference facilities, an art gallery, a library and a conservatory spread over eight levels. The design by Chamberlin, Powell and Bon, provided an extensive foyer with the feeling of a hotel lounge. The theatre, a plain design finished in dark Peruvian walnut, is unusual in that seating is mostly in the stalls, with three circles of just two rows each having short side extensions thrust forward towards the stage. There are no aisles and each row is entered separately through doors that simultaneously woosh closed as the houselights dim. The Royal Shakespeare Company moved productions back and forth continuously between the Barbican and Stratford until 1997 when it decided to play here for only six months of the year, leaving altogether in 2002. The Barbican now stages the Barbican International Theatre Event, which involves theatre and dance companies from all over the world. Abbey Theatre Dublin, Comedie-Francaise and Steppenwolf Theatre Chicago are among the past participants. Cheek By Jowl and Michael Clark Dance have now become resident companies staging regular work here.

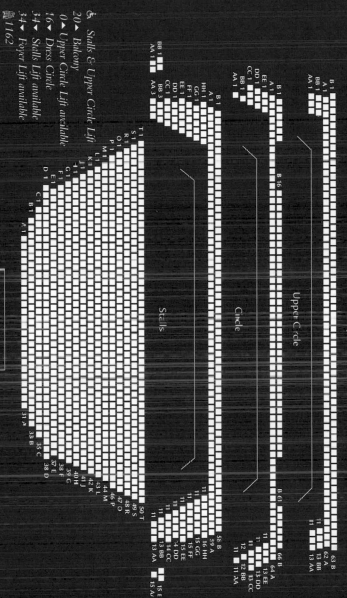

BARBICAN

Gallery

Upper Circle

Circle

Stalls

Stage

   Stalls & Upper Circle Lift
20➤ Balcony
0➤ Upper Circle Lift available
16➤ Dress Circle
34▼ Stalls Lift available
34▼ Foyer Lift available
图1162

Cambridge

Earlham Street, WC2 9HU
Box office: 0870 060 1733
Website: www.rutheatres.com
Tube: Leicester Square/Covent Garden
Train: Charing Cross
Parking: Upper St Martin's Lane/Shelton Street

✳ Air Condition   ◁ Infra-red
♿ Stalls
◉ *Fine Art Deco architectural details.*

When this theatre opened in 1930, the simplicity and modernity of its design by Wimperis, Simpson and Guthrie, with an interior by Serge Chermayeff, was much commented on. The exterior is of undecorated Portland stone, with the unusual corner entrance on Seven Dials rising to an open three sided loggia on its top storey which lies proud of the main building. The auditorium of painted concrete is spanned by plain acoustic arch ribs across the ceiling. There is a gold Art Deco mural of dancers above the doors between the inner and outer foyers, and another in the inner foyer. The diversity of productions it has housed beggars most other venues, with opera, ballet, classical drama, musicals, films and even ice and magic shows. It opened with Beatrice Lilly in the revue *Charlot's Masquerade*. Early visitors included the Comédie Française (1934) but it became a venue for trade film shows by the late 1930s. In 1946 the New London Opera Company was established, presenting its own revivals such as *Don Pasquale*, and visiting Italian and French companies. A return to drama saw the old school *Affairs Of State* (1952) and William Douglas Home's *The Reluctant Debutante* (1955), succeeded by contemporary drama with John Mortimer's first play *The Wrong Side Of The Park* (1960) and Albert Finney making his name as Keith Waterhouse and Willis Hall's *Billy Liar* (1960). Two big musical successes were Tommy Steele in *Half A Sixpence* (1963) and Bruce Forsyth in *Little Me* (1964). These were followed by the last gasp of operetta with John Hanson in *The Desert Song* and *The Student Prince (1968)*. The National Theatre played a season here in 1970 with Maggie Smith in *Hedda Gabler* and Laurence Olivier in *The Merchant Of Venice*. The Cambridge then entered a low period with a seemingly endless succession of musical flops. John Curry's *Theatre Of Skating* (1977) brought ice dancing to the West End and *The Magic Castle* (1984) a Las Vegas style magic show. After closure and refurbishment in 1987 it has been on a more even keel, with the D'Oyly Carte Opera Company launching a comeback with *Iolanthe* and *The Yeomen Of The Guard* (1988), and long runs of the musicals *Return To The Forbidden Planet* (1989), *Fame* (1995), *Grease* (1996) and *Jerry Springer The Opera* (2004). Most recently it has become the venue for *Chicago* (from April 2006) which transferred from the Adelphi.

CAMBRIDGE

Act I • Cambridge

Upper Circle

Dress Circle

Stalls

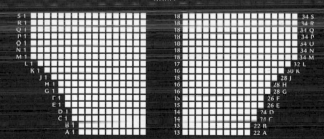

Stage

64▲ Upper Circle, 31▲ Dress Circle, 5▼ Stalls, 0▲ Foyer, 🏛1287

43

Comedy

Panton Street, SW1Y 4DN
Box office: 0870 060 6637
Website: www.theambassadors.com
Tube: Piccadilly Circus/Leicester Square
Train: Charing Cross
Parking: Whitcomb Street/Denman Street
⌁ Infra-red
♿ Dress Circle
⊙ Tiny but charming Royal Room with a fireplace in the vestibule

The Comedy opened in 1881 as the Royal Comedy, but three years later the Royal was removed at the insistence of Buckingham Palace as no official warrant had been issued. Designed by Thomas Verity, the theatre has a pedimented classical façade with a Greek "lady with a lamp" statue in a blind window recess above the entrance. The Renaissance style auditorium was the oldest Victorian auditorium in London until a major refurbishment in 1954. Despite its modest size, the Comedy's original purpose was to present comic opera, and its opening production was *The Mascotte*, an opera comique by Audran. By the early years of the twentieth century however this had given way to drama, courtesy of Sir Frank Benson's company. Actors who have appeared at the Comedy include Herbert Beerbohm Tree, Sarah Bernhardt and Marie Tempest. John Barrymore gave his first London performance here in 1905 and it was here too that Gerald Du Maurier created the role of E W Hornung's *Raffles,* the gentleman burglar (1906). A few years later in 1914 Laurette Taylor had a great success here with *Peg O' My Heart* and throughout World Wars I and II the Comedy staged the revues of C B Cochran and Andre Charlot. In 1956 it became home to the New Watergate Theatre Club, which was set up to produce plays which had been refused a licence by the Lord Chamberlain. It presented Arthur Miller's *A View From The Bridge* (1956) – the opening night of which was attended by Arthur Miller, Marilyn Monroe, Laurence Olivier and Vivien Leigh, Robert Anderson's *Tea And Sympathy* (1957), Tennessee Williams's *Cat On A Hot Tin Roof* (1958) and Peter Shaffer's *Five Finger Exercise* (1958). The high profile support that these productions received helped liberalise attitudes in the censor's office. Since then the Comedy has seen the premieres of a number of other controversial plays including Peter Nichols' *A Day In The Death Of Joe Egg* (1967), *Fortune And Men's Eyes* (1968), David Hare's *Knuckle* (1974), Nell Dunn's *Steaming* (1980), and John Guarre's *Six Degrees Of Separation* (1993). It has also become known as the West End home of Harold Pinter's plays with productions of *The Homecoming* (1991), *The Caretaker* (1992 and 2000), *No Man's Land* (1993), *Moonlight* (1995) and *The Hothouse* (1995).

COMEDY

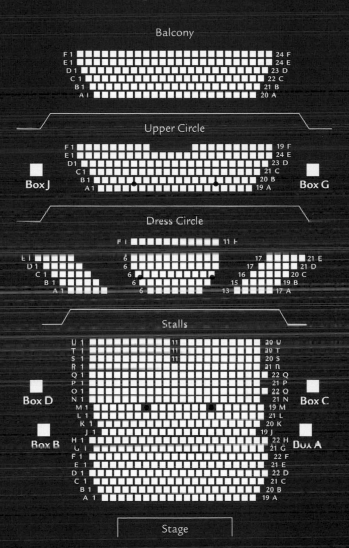

Balcony

```
F 1 ■■■■■■■■■■■■■■■■■■■■■■ 24 F
E 1 ■■■■■■■■■■■■■■■■■■■■■■ 24 E
D 1 ■■■■■■■■■■■■■■■■■■■■■ 23 D
C 1 ■■■■■■■■■■■■■■■■■■■■ 22 C
B 1 ■■■■■■■■■■■■■■■■■■■ 21 B
A 1 ■■■■■■■■■■■■■■■■■■ 20 A
```

Upper Circle

```
         F 1 ■■■■■■■■■       ■■■■■■■■ 19 F
         E 1 ■■■■■■■■■■■■■■■■■■■■■■ 24 E
         D1 ■■■■■■■■■■■■■■■■■■■■■ 23 D
         C 1 ■■■■■■■■■■■■■■■■■■■ 21 C
Box J    B 1 ■■■■■■■■■■■■■■■■■■ 20 B   Box G
         A 1 ■■■■■■■■■■■■■■■■■■ 19 A
```

Dress Circle

```
          F 1 ■■■■■■■■ 11 F
E 1 ■■■■       6 ■■■■■■■■        17 ■■■■ 21 E
D 1 ■■■       6 ■■■■■■■■         17 ■■■ 21 D
C 1 ■■       6 ■■■■■■■■         16 ■■■ 20 C
B 1 ■■       6 ■■■■■■■■        15 ■■■■ 19 B
A 1 ■■      6 ■■■■■■■■        13 ■■■■■ 17 A
```

Stalls

```
         U 1 ■■■■■■■■■■ 11    20 U
         T 1 ■■■■■■■■■■ 11    20 T
         S 1 ■■■■■■■■■■ 11    20 S
         R 1 ■■■■■■■■■■      21 R
         Q 1 ■■■■■■■■■■      22 Q
         P 1 ■■■■■■■■■■      21 P
         O 1 ■■■■■■■■■■      22 O
         N 1 ■■■■■■■■■■      21 N
Box D    M 1 ■■■■■■■■■■      19 M   Box C
         L 1 ■■■■■■■■■■      21 L
         K 1 ■■■■■■■■■■      20 K
         J 1 ■■■■■■■■■■      19 J
Box B    H 1 ■■■■■■■■■■      22 H   Box A
         G 1 ■■■■■■■■■■      21 G
         F 1 ■■■■■■■■■■      22 F
         E 1 ■■■■■■■■■■      21 E
         D 1 ■■■■■■■■■■      22 D
         C 1 ■■■■■■■■■■      21 C
         B 1 ■■■■■■■■■■      20 B
         A 1 ■■■■■■■■■■      19 A
```

Stage

50 ▲ Balcony, 23 ▲ Upper Circle, 0 ▲ Dress Circle
24 ▼ Stalls, 2 ▲ Foyer, ♿ 794

45

Criterion

Criterion

Piccadilly Circus, W1V 9LB
Box office: 0870 060 2313
Website: www.criterion-theatre.co.uk
Tube: Piccadilly Circus
Train: Charing Cross
Parking: Whitcomb Street/Denman Street
♿ Upper Circle
❄ Air Condition ◁ Induction Loop
☉ Unique tiling and mirrors in corridors and stairs.

In 1873 a large restaurant called the Criterion was built on the south side of what was then Regent Circus, on the site of the White Bear, a two hundred year old post inn. A small concert hall was planned for the centre of the building, but at the last minute this was changed to a theatre which duly opened in 1874. Thomas Verity was responsible for the design, which was unique in that it was entirely underground, requiring air to be continuously pumped into it, with only the box office at street level. The classical stone façade is in the second Empire manner while inside the stairs and corridors leading to the bars and auditorium have gilded mirrors and are elaborately tiled with paintings of classical figures and the names of great composers (from when it was to be a concert hall). Initially the theatre was not an unqualified success and in an effort to make it feel less claustrophobic Verity remodelled it in 1883, extending the public areas, and introducing electric lighting and air conditioning for the first time. The final result is considered by some to be the most beautiful theatre in London, with ornate pink and white wedding cake style decoration in the auditorium. From the outset it was established as a home for comedy. Among the great names that have appeared are Mary Moore, Charles Hawtrey, Sybil Thorndyke and Marie Tempest. It has been the launchpad of many careers, witnessing John Gielgud's debut in *Musical Chairs* (1932) and Terence Rattigan's first big success *French Without Tears* (1936). Because of its underground situation the theatre was taken over by the BBC as a radio studio during World War II, and many variety programmes including ITMA were broadcast from here. Theatre returned with Edith Evans in *The Rivals* (1945), Samuel Beckett's *Waiting For Godot* (1955), and Jean Anouilh's *The Waltz Of The Toreadors* (1956), both directed by Peter Hall, transferred here from the Arts Theatre Club. The theatre closed in the late 1980s while the building surrounding it and the adjoining restaurant were demolished and reconstructed, retaining their original façade. Luckily the Criterion emerged not only unscathed but restored, reopening in 1992. The Reduced Shakespeare Company in the *Complete Works Of Shakespeare* (Abridged) (1996) became its longest resident with a 9 year run.

CRITERION

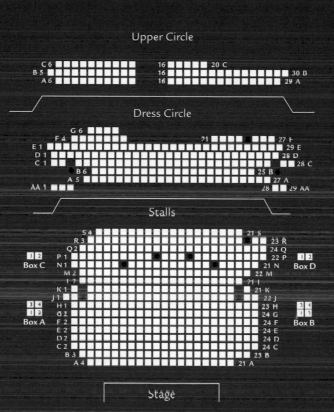

Upper Circle

Dress Circle

Stalls

Stage

Box C
Box D
Box A
Box B

$26\blacktriangledown +10\blacktriangle$ Upper Circle, $32\blacktriangledown$ Dress Circle,
$51\blacktriangledown$ Stalls, $1\blacktriangle$ Foyer, 🏛 598

47

Dominion

Tottenham Court Road W1P 0AQ
Box office: 0870 169 0116
Website: www.livenation.co.uk
Tube: Tottenham Court Road
Train: Charing Cross
Parking: Great Russell Street/Museum Street
♿ Stalls Using Stairlift
◉ Grand mirrored foyer with mezzanine.

This site has variously housed the St Giles Leper Hospital (founded 1101), the Meux brewery (where a twenty two foot high vat of porter ale burst in 1814 drowning eight people), the Court cinema (built 1911), O'Brien's Fun Fair, and finally Luna Park, a venue for thrice daily variety shows. The present building was designed by the brothers William and T R Millburn to operate as both a theatre and cinema and opened in 1929. Although it occupies a whole block, there is only a narrow street frontage with a Portland stone façade in late French Renaissance style. Inside circulation space is generous with twin staircases to a mezzanine, where there was originally a café over the entrance. This leads to a cavernous auditorium graced with the simple lines of a neo–Renaissance picture palace of the 1930s. If the Upper Circle were to be restored it would have 2835 seats, making it the largest theatre in London. Although it opened with the De Sylva, Henderson and Brown stage musical *Follow Through*, starring Elsie Randolph, Ivy Tresmand and Leslie Henson, the Dominion has for most of its life functioned as a super cinema with occasional concerts, and short opera and ballet seasons. During this time a number of prestige films received their first London showing here, beginning with Lon Chaney's sound version of *The Phantom Of The Opera* (1930), and Charlie Chaplin's *City Lights* (1931). In 1958 a huge Todd AO screen and new projection box were installed and the Upper Circle closed off. At that time films enjoyed runs of several years which seem unthinkable today, *South Pacific* (1958-62), *West Side Story* (1962-65), and *The Sound Of Music* (1965-73). Films then alternated with concerts and visits from regional and international opera and ballet companies until 1981 when it reverted to live shows only. The Dominion returned to mainstream theatre use in 1986 with probably the worst example of the '80s mega musical in Dave Clark's *Time*. Following that it was under serious threat of redevelopment which was finally ended and a modest refurbishment was carried out. Shows since then have spanned the good: *Grand Hotel* (1992), the bad: *Bernadette* (1990) and the ugly: *Notre-Dame de Paris* (2000). The most successful were *Grease* (1993), *Disney's Beauty And The Beast* (1996) and *We Will Rock You* (2002) which was due to close in 2006 but has had its stay indefinitely extended due to popular demand..

QUEEN and Ben Elton   NOW IN

49

DOMINION

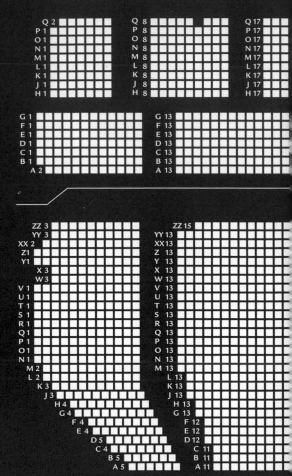

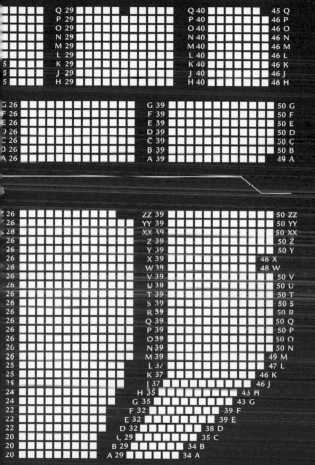

32▲ *Dress Circle,*
10▲ *Stalls,* 0▲ *Foyer,* 🏛 *2182*

Donmar Warehouse

Thomas Neal's, Earlham Street, WC2H 9LD
Box office: 0870 060 6644
Website: www.donmar-warehouse.co.uk
Tube: Leicester Square/Covent Garden
Train: Charing Cross
Parking: Upper St Martin's Lane/Shelton Street
♿ *Stalls Lift available*
✰ *Air Condition* 〈 *Infra-red*
◉ *The West End's only Off Broadway style thrust stage theatre*

The building was originally constructed in the 1870s as the vat room of a brewery, which in 1920 became a film studio – the first in Britain to use colour – before returning to commercial use as a fruit warehouse. The theatre takes its name from a theatre lighting hire company which was once based here, whose name in turn was made up from two names Don(ald) and Mar(got). The Donald in question was Donald Albery the theatre owner, and the Margot, ballerina Margot Fonteyn. They formed a company to produce a ballet season, and when it ended Albery started hiring out the equipment it had purchased. The auditorium was originally used as a rehearsal room, but when the Royal Shakespeare Company was looking for a London space to show productions from its Stratford studio The Other Place, in 1977 a new theatre The Warehouse was born. Despite its cramped and makeshift facilities it rapidly became a very popular venue, staging, amongst others, the original productions of *Piaf* and *Educating Rita*. When the RSC moved to the Barbican in 1982 it was reborn as the Donmar Warehouse. London finally had the equivalent of an Off Broadway theatre – an independent venue available for hire to small producers at a reasonable price. A wide range of work could be seen here and the opportunity was created for touring companies to present their shows in London. Particularly successful were the Show People seasons devoted to the work of American musical theatre writers. The Donmar was then closed and refurbished when the block in which it is located was redeveloped. This brought a layer of designer chic to the previous exposed brickwork, egalitarian bench seating and better technical facilities, but sacrificed some of the rough and ready charm of the place. It reopened in 1992 as a producing venue of limited runs under the direction of the then little known Sam Mendes. Since then a number of landmark productions have transferred to other West End theatres and Broadway including Kander and Ebb's *Cabaret* (1993), Noel Coward's *Design For Living* (1994), Stephen Sondheim's *Company* (1995) and Tom Stoppard's *The Real Thing* (1999) and *Frost/Nixon* (2006). Nicole Kidman appeared here in the sensational production of *The Blue Room* in 1998.

DONMAR WAREHOUSE

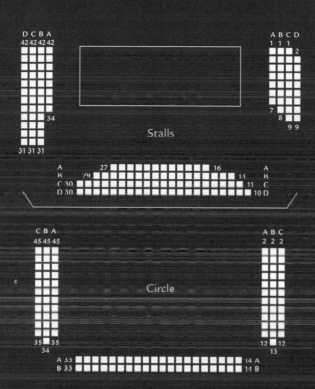

Stalls

Circle

Theatre Royal Drury Lane

Catherine Street, WC2B 5JF
Box office: 0870 890 1109
Website: www.rutheatres.com
Tube: Covent Garden/Holborn/Temple
Train: Charing Cross
 ♿ *Stalls*
 ✱ *Air Condition* ⬦ *Infra-red*
Parking: Drury Lane/Shelton Street
⊙ *The Rotunda and Dress Circle Grand Saloon, and a large collection of paintings, statues and busts throughout the building.*

This is the oldest site in the world in continuous theatrical use. The first theatre was constructed in 1663 to house The King's Servants, one of only two theatre companies granted a royal charter or Patent allowing them to perform plays, after the restoration of Charles II. The entire theatre was the size of the present stage. After it was destroyed by fire, Christopher Wren designed a second building, more than twice the size of the first, which opened in 1674. The fourth and present building, was designed in 1812 by Benjamin Wyatt. Samuel Beazley added the portico in 1820 and the Russell Street colonnade in 1831. The original splendour of the grand staircase, rotunda and saloon are not quite matched by the auditorium redesigned by Emblin Walker, Robert Crombie and Frederick Jones in 1922. This is in Empire style with three large boxes framed by pilasters with columns of imitation lapis lazuli with gilt capitals, and a panelled ceiling with multiple pendant fittings. Most of the greatest British actors have played here, including Nell Gwynne, David Garrick, Henry Irving, Edmund Kean, John Philip Kemble, William Charles Macready, Mrs Siddons, Ellen Terry, Dan Leno and the clown Grimaldi. *Sheridan's School For Scandal* received its premiere in 1777; Kings George I and III both survived assassination attempts at the theatre; ironically it was here too that *God Save The King* was first sung in 1741 and *Rule Britannia* in 1750. It has staged every form of entertainment from Shakespeare through melodrama and opera to pantomime with grand Victorian spectacles offering sinking ships, erupting volcanoes, and earthquakes thrown in for good measure. Noel Coward's *Cavalcade* (1931) featured a cast and crew of over 300. Among Ivor Novello's shows *Glamorous Night* (1935) boasted a liner on fire and *Crest Of The Wave* (1937) a train crash. During World War II it housed the forces' entertainment organisation ENSA. Since then shows have included many Rogers and Hammerstein's musicals, Lerner and Loewe's *My Fair Lady* (1958 and 2001), *42nd Street* (1984), and *Miss Saigon* (1989). *The Producers* (2004) is the theatre's most notable recent success. Now playing host to *Lord of the Rings*, the most expensive West End show ever produced at an estimated cost of £8 million.

Theatre Royal Drury Lane

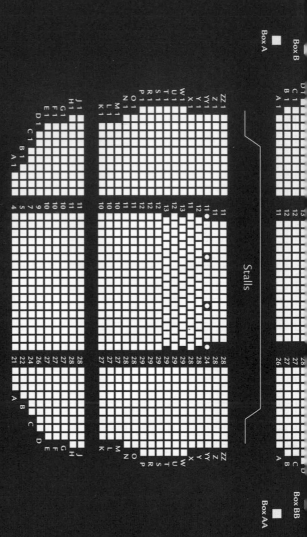

Stalls

90▲ Balcony, 61▲ Upper Circle, 39▲ Dress Circle,
3▲ +20▼ +17▲ Stalls, 6▲ Foyer, ☎ 2237

Box A

Box B

Box AA

Box BB

56

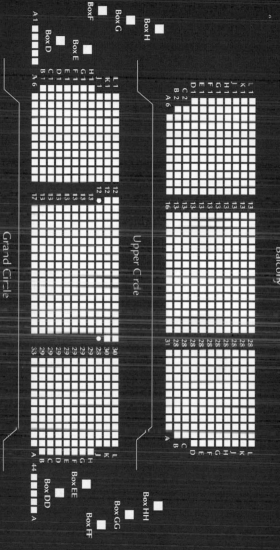

THEATRE ROYAL DRURY LANE
Balcony

Upper Circle

Grand Circle

Box F
Box G
Box H
Box D
Box E
A1
Box J
Box K
Box L
Box M
Box N
Box O
Box P
Box DD
Box EE
Box FF
Box GG
Box HH

57

Duchess

Catherine Street WC2B 5LA
Box office: 0870 890 1103
Website: www.nimaxtheatres.com
Tube: Covent Garden/Holborn/Temple
Train: Charing Cross
✹ Air Condition ⊰ Infra-red
Parking: Drury Lane/Shelton Street
⊙ One of the West End's most intimate theatres.

The Duchess was designed by Ewen Barr and opened in 1929. The awkward nature of the site means that the circle is narrower than the stalls, the foyer and box office are tucked under the circle, and the dressing rooms are stacked onto the auditorium. The modern Tudor Gothic style stone exterior has three bays of windows with enamelled panels containing relief insignia between the floors. The interior by French designers Marc-Henri Levy and Gaston Laverdet was created to avoid visible light fittings and so recessed fixtures provide reflected illumination. The auditorium is fan shaped in a very plain 'moulded' style, the only decoration being a pair of bas-relief panels of figures holding masks above applauding hands by Maurice Lambert between the proscenium and the circle. On the stairs and in the corridors illuminated glass fronted niches were created to contain works of art – nowadays sadly replaced by merchandise. The Duchess holds the record for London's shortest run with *The Intimate Revue* (1930) which failed to reach the end of its first night. Everything that could go wrong did so, creating long gaps between scenes and by midnight, with seven more scenes to go, they cut to the finale – and the next day cancelled the run. Following a production of his play *Laburnum Grove* (1933) J B Priestley became associated with the management and *Eden End* (1934), *Cornelius* (1935), *Time And The Conways* (1937) and *The Linden Tree* (1947) premiered here. Emlyn Williams, who had appeared in the opening production *Tunnel Trench*, returned in *Night Must Fall* (1935) which established him as a writer, and *The Corn Is Green* (1938) with Sybil Thorndyke. T S Eliot's *Murder In The Cathedral* (1936) made its West End debut here, as did Terence Rattigan's *The Deep Blue Sea* (1952) and many Harold Pinter plays from *The Caretaker* (1960) to *Other Places* (1985). It has seen many transfers from other theatres including Noel Coward's *Blithe Spirit* (1942) which ran for 1997 performances (London's longest run before *The Mousetrap*), Bill Naughton's *Alfie* (1963), *Oh! Calcutta* (1974) – which ran for six years, *No Sex Please We're British* (1986), and *Don't Dress For Dinner* (1992).

DUCHESS

H 1 — 22 H
G 1 — 20 G
F 1 — 20 F
E 1 — 20 E
D 1 — 20 D

C 1 — 20 C
B 1 — 20 B
A 1 — 20 A

Stalls

O 1 — 15 — 29 O
N 2 — 15 — 28 N
M 1 — 15 — 29 M
L 1 — 15 — 28 L
K 1 — 14 — 26 K
J 1 — 13 — 24 J
H 1 — 12 — 23 H
G 1 — 11 — 24 G
F 1 — 22 F
E 1 — 18 E
D 1 — 17 D
C 1 — 16 C
B 1 — 15 B
A 1 — 14 A

Stage

12▲ Dress Circle, 21▼ Stalls, 1▲ Foyer, 🎭 *476*

Duke of York's

St Martin's Lane WC2N 4BG
Box office: 0870 060 6623
Website: www.theambassadors.com
Tube: Leicester Square/Charing Cross
Train: Charing Cross
♿ *Dress Circle* ◀ *Infra-red*
Parking: Upper St Martin's Lane/Bedfordbury
◉ *Dress Circle bar offers access to first floor loggia.*

Opening in 1892 as the Trafalgar Square Theatre, it was designed by Walter Emden with the novelty of real open fires in the auditorium. The name was changed to the Duke Of York's in 1895 to honour the future King George V. The exterior is of painted brick and stone with a small central open loggia at first floor level. Owing to the restricted width of the site the auditorium is narrow and deep and supporting pillars originally created a large number of restricted view seats. These pillars were removed in a major refurbishment in 1979 that restored the original decorative scheme of cream, gold and russet. Unusually there is no formal proscenium arch, the stage opening simply being defined by the pillars supporting the stage boxes. Among the audiences to have seen David Belasco's one act curtain-raiser *Madame Butterfly* (1900) was Puccini, who was inspired to write his opera of the same name. J M Barrie had a long association with the theatre, which started with *The Admirable Crichton* (1902). This was a success despite a strike by the stage staff on the first night, with the result that the cast, which included Gerald du Maurier, had to move the scenery themselves. Peter Pan made his stage debut here in 1904 and returned every Christmas until 1914, with Noel Coward playing *Slightly Soiled* in 1912. Other Barrie plays produced here were *What Every Woman Knows* (1908), *Old Friends*, *The Twelve Pound Look* and *Rosalind*. Coward returned to premiere the revues *London Calling* (1923) with Gertrude Lawrence, *Easy Virtue* (1926), *Home Chat* (1927) and *Waiting In The Wings* (1960). Other important plays to receive their first performances here were Henrik Ibsen's *The Master Builder* and George Bernard Shaw's *Misalliance*. The actor's union Equity was formed as a result of a meeting held here by a group of actors in 1920. Landmark productions of more recent years include Orson Welles's *Moby Dick* (1955), Frank Marcus's *The Killing Of Sister George* (1965), Alan Ayckbourn's first major success *Relatively Speaking* (1967) and Richard Harris's *Stepping Out* (1984). A long association with the Royal Court Theatre has seen many transfers, including Ariel Dorfman's *Death And The Maiden* (1992), David Mamet's *Oleanna* (1993) and Tom Stoppard's *Rock'n'Roll* (2006).

DUKE OF YORK'S

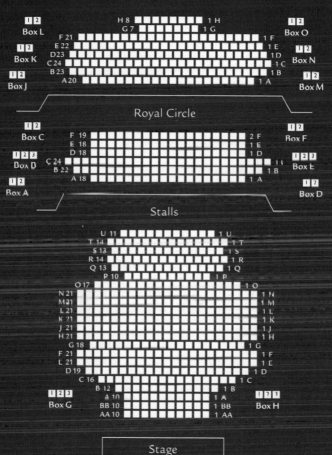

Upper Circle

Box L | Box O
Box K | Box N
Box J | Box M

H 8 — 1 H
G 7 — 1 G
F 21 — 1 F
E 22 — 1 E
D 23 — 1 D
C 24 — 1 C
B 23 — 1 B
A 20 — 1 A

Royal Circle

Box C | Box F
Box D | Box E
Box A | Box D

F 19 — 2 F
E 18 — 1 E
D 18 — 1 D
C 24 — 1 C
B 22 — 1 B
A 18 — 1 A

Stalls

U 11 — 1 U
T 14 — 1 T
S 13 — 1 S
R 14 — 1 R
Q 13 — 1 Q
P 10 — 1 P
O 17 — 1 O
N 21 — 1 N
M 21 — 1 M
L 21 — 1 L
K 21 — 1 K
J 21 — 1 J
H 21 — 1 H
G 18 — 1 G
F 21 — 1 F
E 21 — 1 E
D 19 — 1 D
C 16 — 1 C
B 12 — 1 B
A 10 — 1 A
BB 10 — 1 BB
AA 10 — 1 AA

Box G | Box H

Stage

23 ▲ *Upper Circle,* 0 ▲ *Dress Circle,* 20 ▼ *Stalls,* 0 ▲ *Foyer,* 🏛 ᶜ*650*

61

Fortune

Russell Street, WC2B 5HH
Box office: 0870 060 6626
Website: www.theambassadors.com
Tube: Covent Garden/Holborn/Temple
Train: Charing Cross
Parking: Drury Lane/Shelton Street
✱ *Air Condition*
◉ *The most intimate West End theatre almost feels like a private house.*

The first West End theatre to be built after World War I stands on the site of the Albion Tavern, a haunt of Georgian and Victorian actors and writers. It was originally to be called the Crown as it is 'grafted onto' the Scottish National Church in Crown Court, with an entrance passageway passing through its entire depth on the left hand side, and the church hall beneath it. The opening production was appropriately (or inappropriately) a play called *Sinners*. Designed by Ernest Schaufelberg in 1924 it is a radical departure from previous theatres, without fully embracing the Art Deco style of those that came soon after. It is a plain square building of brick and stucco, its windows giving a hint of the Medieval, the only external decoration being a statue of Fortune high above the entrance – although this is claimed to be Terpsichore the Greek Muse of dancing by some. Original ornamental doors give way to the marble and copper foyer with a brass plate bearing the Shakespearean inscription "There is a tide in the affairs of men which, taken at the flood, leads on to Fortune". The auditorium is remarkably intimate, containing about the same number of seats as the balcony of Drury Lane whose stage door it faces. The restricted size of both the stage and the auditorium has dictated the shows it has presented. Its early days saw a number of undistinguished plays, with Frederick Lonsdale's *On Approval* (1927) its first success. The People's National Theatre run by Nancy Price established itself here in 1930, presenting John Galsworthy's first play *The Silver Box* (1931). During World War II it was taken over by the services' entertainment organisation ENSA which was based in Drury Lane. After the war, *Power Without Glory* (1947) brought two unknowns, Dirk Bogarde and Kenneth More, to the West End. Two revues, Michael Flanders and Donald Swan's *At The Drop Of A Hat* (1957) and *Beyond The Fringe* (1961) with Alan Bennett, Peter Cook, Jonathan Miller and Dudley Moore, defined the times in which they were presented. Long running transfers of Peter Shaffer's *Sleuth* (1973), Vivian Ells's *Mr Cinders* (1983) and Susan Hill's record-breaking *The Woman In Black* (1990) have also been important in their genres.

FORTUNE

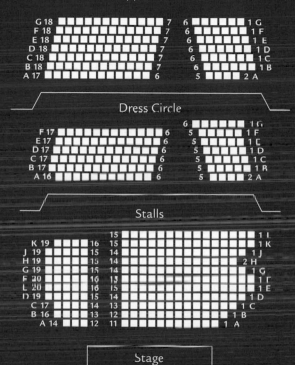

Upper Circle

G 18		7		6		1 G
F 18		7		6		1 F
E 18		7		6		1 E
D 18		7		6		1 D
C 18		7		6		1 C
B 18		7		6		1 B
A 17		6		5		2 A

Dress Circle

F 17		6		6		1 G
E 17		6		5		1 F
D 17		6		5		1 E
C 17		6		5		1 D
B 17		6		5		1 C
A 16		6		5		1 B
				5		2 A

Stalls

	15		15		1 L
K 19	16	15		1 K
J 19	15	14		1 J
H 19	15	14		2 H
G 19	15	14		1 G
F 20	16	13		1 F
L 20	16	15		1 E
D 19	15	14		1 D
C 17	14	13		1 C
B 16	13	12		1 B
A 14	12	11		1 A

Stage

Garrick

Charing Cross Road WC2H oHH
Box office: 0870 890 1104
Website: www.nimaxtheatres.com
Tube: Leicester Square/Charing Cross
Train: Charing Cross
Parking: Lisle Street/Bedfordbury
♿ *Dress Circle* ♪ *Infra-red*
◉ *A copy of a lost Gainsborough portrait of the actor manager David Garrick adorns the wooden panelled foyer bar.*

The building was financed by W S Gilbert – of 'and Sullivan' fame – and designed by Walter Emden, with contributions by C J Phipps. Construction was almost abandoned half-way through when excavations uncovered an underground river. Gilbert is said to have remarked that he did not know "whether to go on with the building or let the fishing rights". It was the first British theatre to be named after an actor. The distinctive curved Portland and Bath stone frontage incorporates a colonnaded loggia at first floor level that can be reached via the Dress Circle bar. The auditorium is decorated in Italian Renaissance style in cream and red, with Cupids holding laurel decked shields decorating the plasterwork on the balcony fronts. As at the Duke of York's there is no formal proscenium arch, the stage opening simply being defined by the supporting pillars of the stage boxes. The Garrick eventually opened in 1889 with Pinero's *The Profligate*, followed by his *Lady Bountiful* (1891), *The Notorious Mrs Ebbsmith* (1895), and *Iris* (1901) and it has mostly been associated with comedies. In 1934 an unsuccessful attempt was made to revive Old Time Music Hall and shortly after this plans were announced for its rebuilding as a super cinema but the scheme never materialised. Walter Greenwood's *Love On The Dole* (1935) was a great success that established both the theatre and Wendy Hiller its star. In the 1940s ex Aldwych farceurs – performers Robertson Hare and Robert Drayton, and writers Vernon Sylvane and Ben Travers – moved in with *Warn That Man (1941)*, *Aren't Men Beasts* (1942), *She Follows Me About* (1943) and *Madame Louise (1945)*. After the World War II Jack Buchanan assumed direction of the theatre, appearing in Frederick Lonsdale's *Canaries Sometimes Sing* (1947), and Sylvaines's *As Long As They're Happy* (1953). He also presented Yolande Donlan in Garson Kanin's *Born Yesterday* (1947) directed by Laurence Olivier, and *To Dorothy A Son* (1951). In 1967 Brian Rix moved his company here from the Whitehall with farces such as *Stand By Your Bedouin* and *Don't Just Lie There Say Something*. *No Sex Please We're British* (1982) transferred for a four year run, the theatre's longest until the transfer of the National Theatre production of J B Priestley's *An Inspector Calls* (1995) which ran until 2001.

GARRICK

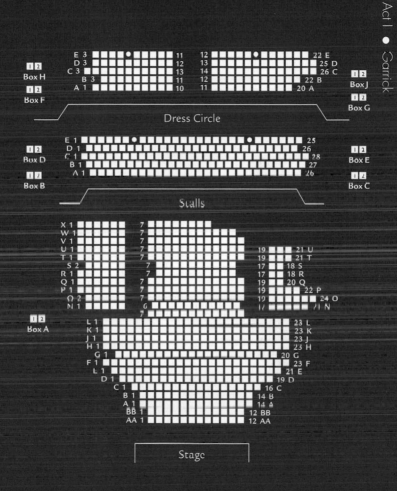

Box H   1 2
Box F   1 2

E 3 ▪▪▪▪▪▪▪● ▪▪▪ 11
D 3 ▪▪▪▪▪▪▪▪▪▪ 12
C 3 ▪▪▪▪▪▪▪▪▪ 13
B 3 ▪▪▪▪▪▪▪▪▪ 11
A 1 ▪▪▪▪▪▪▪▪▪ 10

12 ▪▪▪▪▪▪▪▪▪ 22 E
13 ▪▪▪▪▪▪▪▪ 25 D
14 ▪▪▪▪▪▪▪▪ 26 C
12 ▪▪▪▪▪▪▪▪ 22 B
11 ▪▪▪▪▪▪▪▪ 20 A

Box J   1 2
Box G   1 2

Dress Circle

Box D   1 2
Box B   1 2

E 1 ▪▪▪▪▪●▪▪▪▪▪▪●▪▪ 25
D 1 ▪▪▪▪▪▪▪▪▪▪▪▪ 26
C 1 ▪▪▪▪▪▪▪▪▪▪▪ 28
B 1 ▪▪▪▪▪▪▪▪▪▪▪ 27
A 1 ▪▪▪▪▪▪▪▪▪▪ 26

Box E   1 2
Box C   1 2

Stalls

Box A   1 2

X 1 ▪▪▪▪▪ 7
W 1 ▪▪▪▪▪ 7
V 1 ▪▪▪▪▪ 7
U 1 ▪▪▪▪▪ 7
T 1 ▪▪▪▪▪ 7
S 2 ▪▪▪▪▪ 7
R 1 ▪▪▪▪▪ 7
Q 1 ▪▪▪▪▪ 7
P 1 ▪▪▪▪▪ 7
O 2 ▪▪▪▪▪ 7
N 1 ▪▪▪▪▪ 6
7

19 ▪▪ 21 U
19 ▪▪ 21 T
17 ▪▪ 18 S
17 ▪▪ 18 R
19 ▪▪ 20 Q
19 ▪▪ 22 P
19 ▪▪ 24 O
17 ▪▪ 21 N

L 1 ▪▪▪▪▪▪▪▪▪▪▪▪ 23 L
K 1 ▪▪▪▪▪▪▪▪▪▪▪▪ 23 K
J 1 ▪▪▪▪▪▪▪▪▪▪▪ 23 J
H 1 ▪▪▪▪▪▪▪▪▪▪▪ 23 H
G 1 ▪▪▪▪▪▪▪▪▪▪ 20 G
F 1 ▪▪▪▪▪▪▪▪▪▪ 23 F
E 1 ▪▪▪▪▪▪▪▪▪ 21 E
D 1 ▪▪▪▪▪▪▪▪ 19 D
C 1 ▪▪▪▪▪▪▪ 16 C
B 1 ▪▪▪▪▪▪ 14 B
A 1 ▪▪▪▪▪▪ 14 A
BB 1 ▪▪▪▪▪ 12 BB
AA 1 ▪▪▪▪▪ 12 AA

Stage

SAFETY

Garrick

Gielgud

Shaftesbury Avenue, W1V 8AR
Box office: 0870 950 0915
Website: www.delfont-mackintosh.com
Tube: Piccadilly Circus
Train: Charing Cross
  ♿ *Dress Circle*
✱*Air Condition* ◄ *Infra-red*
Parking: Brewer Street/Denman Street
◉ *A bust of John Gielgud in the Foyer.*

Designed by W G R Sprague, the Hicks Theatre opened in 1906, but was known as the Globe from 1909, before becoming the Gielgud in 1994. Like the Novello and the Aldwych, also designed by Sprague, it bookends a whole block with the Queen's Theatre. The four storey Edwardian Baroque façade in Portland stone surmounted by a domed turret makes the most of its corner site. The Dress Circle bar has an oval gallery from which patrons can look down on the foyer, as at the Aldwych. The auditorium is in Louis XVI style, with Corinthian columns framing the boxes and an allegorical cartouche above the proscenium. Actor manager Seymour Hicks built and named the theatre, and he, together with his wife Ellaline Terriss, appeared in the opening production, a musical play *The Beauty Of Bath,* which transferred from the Aldwych. Star names, often in not very distinguished plays or comedies, and star-laden revivals have been its staple fare. The management of actress Marie Lohr and husband Anthony Prinsep raised the standards with Somerset Maugham's *Our Betters* (1923), Frederick Lonsdale's *Aren't We All?* (1923) and Noel Coward's *Fallen Angels* (1925). Probably its heyday came when the H M Tennant management established its headquarters in the building, producing a succession of classic revivals both in house and at other theatres. The first were George Bernard Shaw's *Candida* (1937), Somerset Maughan's *The Constant Wife* (1937) and Oscar Wilde's *The Importance Of Being Earnest* (1939), directed by and starring John Gielgud, with Edith Evans giving the definitive performance as Lady Bracknell. Important new plays were Christopher Fry's *The Lady's Not For Burning* (1949), Fry's translation of Jean Anouilh's *Ring Round The Moon* with Paul Schofield as good and bad twins, Noel Coward's *Nude With Violin* (1956), and Robert Bolt's *A Man For All Seasons* (1960), also starring Paul Schofield. Many of Alan Ayckbourn's plays had their London premiere here: *The Norman Conquests* trilogy starring Tom Courtenay (1974), *Ten Times Table* (1978), *Man Of The Moment* (1989), *Communicating Doors* (1995) and *Things We Do For Love* (1998). The Royal Shakespeare Company has staged seasons including *All's Well That Ends Well* (2004), *The Crucible* and *The Canterbury Tales* (2006).

GIELGUD

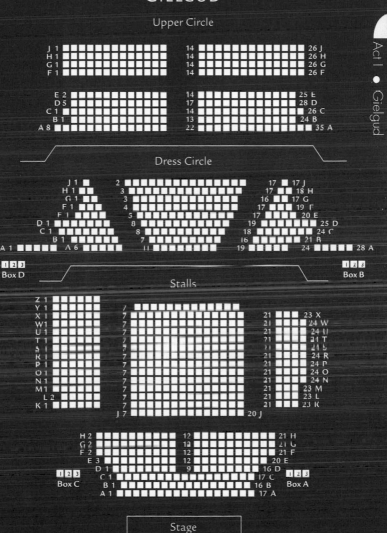

35▲ Upper Circle, 3▲ Dress Circle, 3▲ + 22▼ Stalls, 1▲ Foyer, ♿888

Theatre Royal Haymarket

Haymarket, SW1Y 4HT
Box office: 0870 400 0626
Website: www.trh.co.uk
Tube: Piccadilly Circus/Charing Cross
Train: Charing Cross
&. *Stalls*
✼ *Air Condition*
Parking: Whitcomb Street/Trafalgar Square
◉ *The elegant mirrored vestibule at rear of the Dress Circle.*

The Little Theatre In The Hay opened without a license in 1720 on a site adjoining the present building, and continued in this manner when a group of actors who broke away from the Drury Lane company, calling themselves 'The Comedians Of His Majesty's Revels' took it over. The crude satires performed under the management of Henry Fielding resulted in the introduction of theatre censorship in 1737. Eventually in 1766 under the management of Samuel Foote it became the third theatre to be granted a royal patent. The rumbustious nature of theatregoing in earlier times is demonstrated by two incidents which took place here. At a Royal Command performance in 1794 the crowd was so great that 20 people were crushed to death in a stampede. In 1805 the Tailors Riot occurred when hundreds of tailors, enraged by a satire on their trade, barracked a performance and troops were called to disperse them. The present building designed by John Nash, in classical style stucco with a Corinthian portico was constructed in 1821, and opened with Sheridan's *The Rivals*. The interior was remodelled in 1880 by C J Phipps, creating the first proscenium arch in the form of a four sided gold picture frame, and again in 1904 by C Stanley Peach in an elaborate Louis XVI style, restored in 1994. The name Theatre Royal Haymarket was assumed in 1855. Between 1853 and 1878 John Buckstone presented more than 150 productions. Actor manager Herbert Beerbohm Tree took over in 1887, and *Hamlet* and *Trilby* (1895) were so successful that he built Her Majesty's theatre opposite from the profits. Among plays to premiere here were Oscar Wilde's *A Woman Of No Importance* (1893) and Ibsen's *Ghosts* (1914). During World War II an H M Tennant/John Gielgud repertory season was presented with *Hamlet, A Midsummer Night's Dream, Love For Love, The Duchess Of Malfi* and *The Circle*. In recent times, there have been successful revivals including Vanessa Redgrave in *Lady Windermere's Fan* (2002) and Judi Dench in *Hay Fever* (2006). It has recently been announced in the press that the Haymarket has formed a company to present its own productions. The first season of works is to be directed by the former Artistic Director of the Almeida, Jonathan Kent and could provide a possible blueprint for a more innovative the West End theatre.

THEATRE ROYAL HAYMARKET

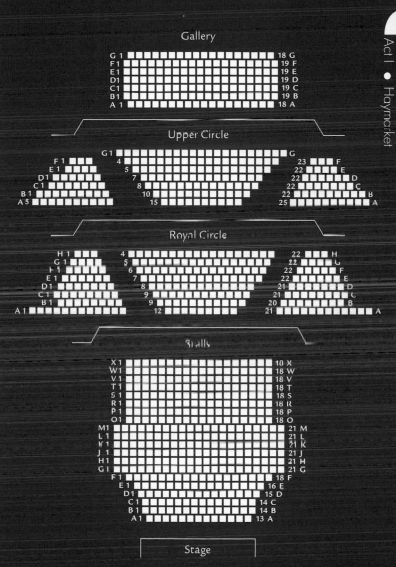

Gallery

Upper Circle

Royal Circle

Stalls

Stage

64▲ Upper Circle, 28▲ Dress Circle, 20▼ +11▲ Stalls, 3▲ Foyer, ♿888

Her Majesty's

Haymarket, SW1Y 4QR
Box office: 020 7494 5400
Website: www.rutheatres.com
Tube: Piccadilly Circus/Charing Cross
Train: Charing Cross
♿ *Stalls*
❅ *Air Condition* ◁ *Infra-red*
Parking: Whitcomb Street/Trafalgar Square
◉ *The panelled foyer with a carved and painted ceiling.*

The first theatre on this site, designed by John Vanburgh to house a company formed by William Congreve, opened in 1705 as the Queen's. After Handel staged his first opera in England, *Rinaldo* (1711), he received Royal patronage to establish a company, and it became the first theatre devoted entirely to Italian opera. Despite staging the first oratorio in England and other Handel operas it was not financially successful. The second theatre opened as the King's in 1791, and continued to present Italian opera and romantic ballet, changing its name to Her Majesty's Theatre, Italian Opera House in 1837, before dropping the Italian Opera House a decade later. English premieres included Mozart's *Cosi Fan Tutte* (1811), *The Magic Flute (*1811), *The Marriage Of Figaro* (1812) and *Don Giovanni* (1817), Beethoven's *Fidelio (*1851), Bizet's *Carmen* (1878) and the complete cycle of Wagner's *The Ring* (1882). After a further fire in 1867 a third theatre was reconstructed within the shell, but it was never really successful. The current building designed by C J Phipps for actor manager Herbert Beerbohm Tree opened in 1897. The façade is in Portland stone, with a first floor loggia, and crowned with a copper clad dome. The interior is Louis XV style, containing marble Corinthian columns and a painted ceiling, and featuring the first flat stage floor in Britain. Between 1897 and 1914 Tree staged eighteen sumptuous Shakespeare productions, and played Higgins to Mrs Patrick Campbell's Eliza in the premiere of George Bernard Shaw's *Pygmalion* (1914). In 1904 Tree started a drama school in the suite of rooms in the dome, which eventually became the Royal Academy of Dramatic Art, moving in 1905 to its present home in Gower Street. An abrupt change of management brought in the musical *Chu Chin Chow* (1916) whose record five year run remained unchallenged for nearly forty years. Since World War II Her Majesty's has presented a succession of great musicals, including *Brigadoon* (1949), *Paint Your Wagon* (1953), *West Side Story* (1958) and *Fiddler On The Roof* (1967). *Live from Her Majesty's* was a variety show which ran for three seasons on ITV from 1982 to 1985 and it was during a performance that Tommy Cooper collapsed and died in 1984. *The Phantom Of The Opera* (1986) is still in residence, making it one of the West End's longest running productions.

HER MAJESTY'S

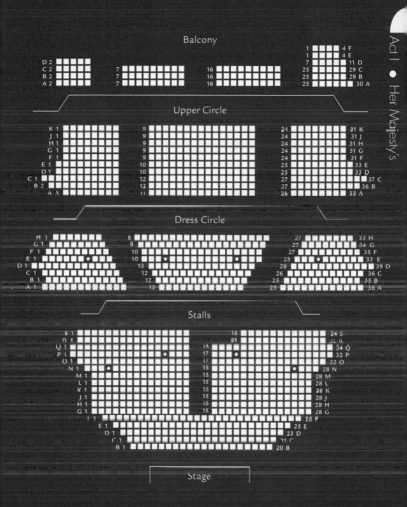

Balcony

Upper Circle

Dress Circle

Stalls

Stage

89 ▲ Balcony, 62 ▲ Upper Circle, 32 ▲ Dress Circle, 22 ▼ +18 ▲ Stalls,
0 ▲ Foyer, 🚻 1219

London Coliseum

St Martin's Lane, WC2N 4ES
Box office: 020 7632 8300
Website: www.eno.org
Tube: Leicester Square/Charing Cross
Train: Charing Cross
♧ *Stalls*
〈 *Infra-red*
Parking: Upper St Martin's Lane/Bedfordbury
◉ *The "revolving" globe on its tower is one of London's landmark sights.*

London's largest theatre, designed by Frank Matcham on the instruction of Oswald Stoll to be its grandest variety house, opened in 1904 as the London Coliseum. The Italian Renaissance exterior style is faced in terracotta, with balconied windows set in loggias on the second floor, surmounted by a tower with a globe on top. This globe originally revolved, but after a protracted dispute with the local council, it remained fixed with lights installed inside which give the impression of movement. Figures at the base of the tower represent Art, Music, Science and Literature. There was a roof garden refreshment room under a glass and iron conservatory roof, which was demolished in 1951. The revolving globe and rooftop conservatory were reinstated in a restoration completed in 2004. The lavishly decorated auditorium is unusual in that the circles do not overhang the stalls. Matcham's design employed the latest technology including the world's first revolving stage, in three concentric rings of 25ft, 50ft and 75ft diameter, capable of moving in either direction. This allowed the staging of horse and chariot races against the movement for the revolve among the theatre's many spectaculars. There were four shows daily at noon, 3pm, 6pm and 9pm, presenting two different programmes, so that patrons could see one, take tea on the roof and be entertained by a band in the hour-long interval, and then see the second. The initial expense was so great that the original company failed after two years. Stoll bought it back and reopened it successfully with all manner of attractions, including music hall stars, performing animals and circus acts, mixed with legitimate acts such as Ellen Terry performing excerpts from *The Merchant Of Venice*, Sarah Bernhardt, Lillie Langtry, and Diaghilev's Russian Ballet. The first public demonstration of television was staged here in 1930. The name was shortened to the Coliseum in 1931 when it became a regular theatre with the opening of *White Horse Inn*. It saw the London premieres of many of the great American shows such as *Annie Get Your Gun* (1947), *Kiss Me Kate* (1951), *Guys And Dolls* (1953) and *The Pajama Game* (1955). Times changed, its size became a problem, and it was converted to a cinema in 1963 before finally closing. Fortunately it staved off demolition and in 1968 became home to what is now the English National Opera and is home to the English National Ballet's Christmas season each year.

LONDON COLISEUM

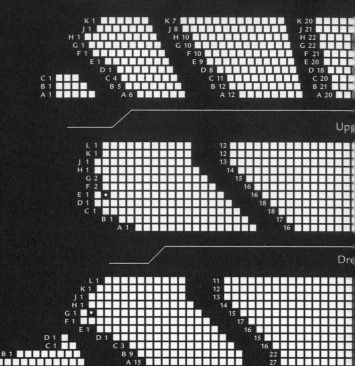

Upp

Dre

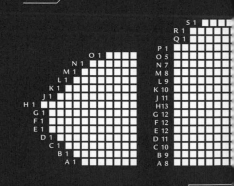

76

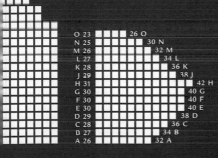

68▲ Balcony, 56▲ Upper Circle, 33▲ Dress Circle 2▼ Stalls, 0▲ Foyer, ♟2,358

LONDON PALLADIUM

U

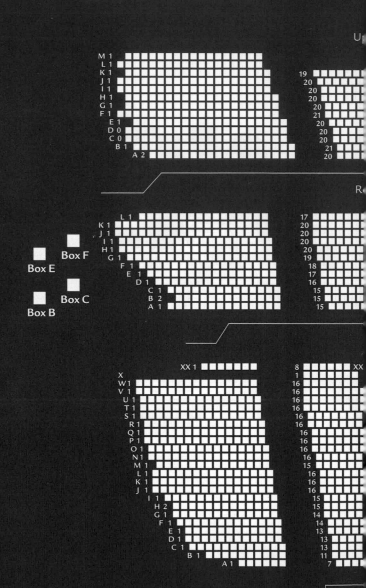

R

Box F

Box E

Box C

Box B

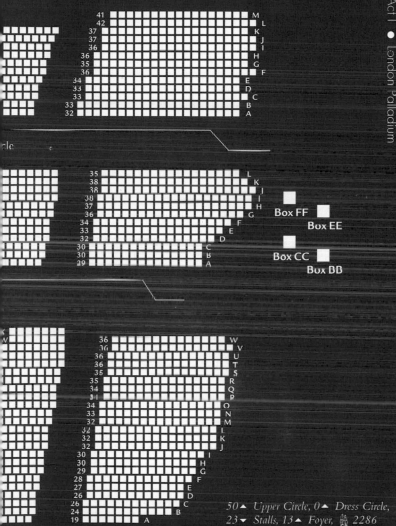

Lyceum

Wellington Street WC2E 7DA
Box office: 0870 243 9000
Website: www.livenation.co.uk
Tube: Covent Garden/Holborn/Temple
Train: Charing Cross
♿ Stalls
✲ Air Condition 〈 Infra-red
Parking: Drury Lane/Shelton Street
◉ Elaborately painted murals in the auditorium.

The Lyceum opened in 1772 as a space for exhibitions, concerts and lectures, as well as hosting circus and other events. When Drury Lane burnt down in 1809 the company transferred, taking their theatre license with them, to the renamed Theatre Royal Lyceum. It became the Theatre Royal English Opera House when they moved back to Drury Lane, once again unable to present plays. The original Lyceum was itself then destroyed by fire and was replaced with a Samuel Beazley designed building which opened in 1834. It presented opera, burletta and other entertainments until the monopoly of Patent theatres was broken in 1843, and eventually became known as the Royal Lyceum Theatre. When the Covent Garden burnt down in 1856, its company moved in until their theatre was rebuilt. Plays began to be presented and in 1871 Henry Irving first appeared here in *The Bells*, a sensation which he followed with *The Pickwick Papers*. Irving took over the theatre in 1878 and appeared in melodramas and lavish Shakespeare productions, with Ellen Terry as his leading lady, until a final performance as Shylock in 1902. The building was in a poor condition and was demolished, except for the façade and portico, and replaced by the current theatre, which was designed as a music hall by Bertie Crew in 1904. The interior, in a lavish baroque style with painted panels was likened to a brothel. Unable to stand the competition from the Coliseum, it was acquired by the Melville brothers in 1909, who switched to a formula of melodrama, mostly written by themselves, combined with annual pantomimes. This later broadened out into opera and ballet again. It was sold for development in 1938 and finally closed with John Gielgud as Hamlet in 1939 uttering a curtain speech cry of "Long live the Lyceum!". For thirty years from 1945 it was used as a dance hall before finally closing again. A season of the National Theatre's promenade production of *The Mysteries* (1982) reawakened interest, and after many near misses it was restored and reopened with *Jesus Christ Superstar* in 1996. Since 1999 The Lyceum has been the home for The Disney corporation's lavish adaptation of *The Lion King*.

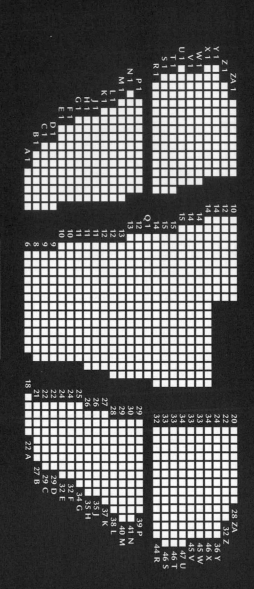

Stalls

Stage

85 ▲ Upper Circle, 32 ▲ Dress Circle
7 ▼ Stalls, 3 ▲ Foyer, ⓘ 1,899

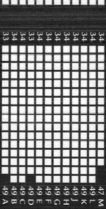

LYCEUM

Upper Circle

Royal Circle

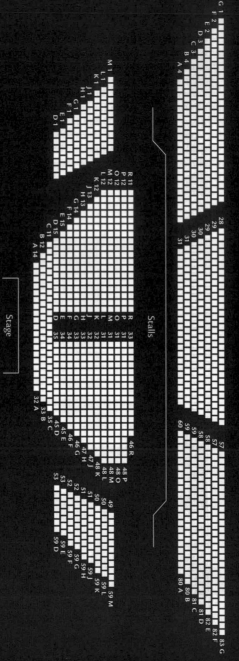

OLIVIER

Circle

Stalls

Stage

Olivier – ♿ *Stalls Lift available,* ▲ *93 Dress Circle Lift available,* ▲ *49 Stalls Lift available,* 0 ▲ *Foyer,* 🍽 *1,160*

LYTTELTON

Circle

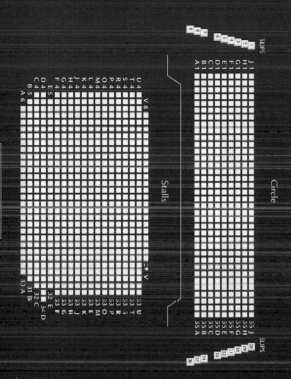

SLIPS

J 1
H 1
G 1
F 1
E 1
D 1
C 1
B 1
A 1

1
2
3
4
5
6
7
8
9

SLIPS

35 J
35 H
35 G
35 F
35 E
35 D
35 C
35 B
35 A

28
29
30
31
32
33
34
35

Stalls

Stage

U 4
T 4
S 4
R 4
P 4
O 4
M 4
L 4
K 4
J 4
H 4
G 4
F 4
E 5
D 4
C 4
B 5
A 6

V 8

33 U
33 T
33 S
33 R
33 P
33 O
33 M
33 L
33 K
33 J
33 H
33 G
33 F
33 E

29 V

33 A
31 B
32 C
32 D
32 E

Lyttelton – ♿ *Stalls,* ▲ *22 Dress Circle Lift available, 0▲ Stalls, 0▼ Foyer,* 🚻 *9C0*

91

New London

Drury Lane, WC2B 5PW
Box office: 0870 890 0141
Website: www.rutheatres.com
Tube: Holborn/Covent Garden
Train: Charing Cross
Parking: Beneath the theatre
❄ Air Condition   ◁ Infra- red

Although the present building is one of the few post World War II theatres in London, it occupies a site of taverns and other entertainment establishments dating back to the time of Nell Gwynne, who lived nearby. The Mogul Saloon opened here in 1847 and enjoyed considerable popularity as a music hall, being renamed the Middlesex Music Hall in 1851. It was rebuilt on a grander scale in 1891 before Oswald Stoll took it over and rebuilt it in 1911 as the New Middlesex Theatre of Varieties. This was a grand design by Frank Matcham, possessing the largest frontage of any theatre in London, with an Arabesque style interior. It continued throughout World War I, and was the last music hall in London to retain a Chairman. A new management in 1919 redecorated it in French style, renamed it the Winter Garden and opened it as a theatre. A succession of musical comedies by writers such as P G Wodehouse and George Gershwin established it as a success in its new role. However after Sophie Tucker in Vivian Ellis's *Follow A Star* (1930) and Gracie Fields in *Walk This Way* (1932) it went into decline, often dark for long periods. Alastair Sim appeared here as Captain Hook in *Peter Pan* (1942) for the first time, a role he continued to play for 26 years. It closed in 1959 and was sold for redevelopment, but although it was demolished in 1965, planning wrangles ensured that construction did not start until the 1970s. The New London theatre opened in 1973 with no real street frontage, as part of a scheme that included a restaurant, offices, shops and flats. Paul Turtkovic, in association with stage designer Sean Kenny, designed it to be flexible, able to be configured in both proscenium arch and theatre in the round formats, with almost one third of the floor area built on a revolve. Enabling it to accommodate any kind of production was supposed to be more attractive to producers, but despite a variety of productions, including Richard Gere in *Grease* (1973), it proved no more successful than before, and became a television studio in 1977. Then came a show that could take advantage of the theatre's flexibility – *Cats* (1981), which closed on its 21st birthday as London's longest running musical and was succeeded by another unconventional show *Blue Man Group* (2005). In late 2007 the theatre is to be the venue for the RSC's productions of *King Lear* and *The Seagull* starring Ian McKellen and directed by Trevor Nunn and this is to be followed in 2008 by a musical adaptation of *Gone with the Wind*.

New London

Dress Circle

E 1   37 E
D 1   40 D
C 1   41 C
B 5   44 B
A 7   43 A

B 1   4 B   B 45   48
A 1   6 A   A 44

Orchestra Stalls

U 1   37 U
T 1   40 T
S 1   41 S
R 5   44 R
P 7   43 P
O 9   44 O
N 11   43 N
M 13   34 M
L 14   30 L
K 14   29 K
J 15   29 J

O 1   8 O   R 45
N 1   10 N   P 44
M 1   12 M   O 45
L 1   13 L   N 44
K 1   13 K   M 35
J 1   14 J   L 31
I 1   14 I   K 30
     J 30
     I 30

H 1   12 H
G 1   G 2   18 G   24 F
H 1   F 5   20 F   27 E
E 1   E 7   21 E   30 D
D 1   D 9   22 D   31 C
C 1   C 10   22 C   30 B
B 3   B 11   22 B
A 5   A 11   21 A   27 A

Stage

0 ▲ *Foyer,* 🛗 *1102,*
Escalator ▲ *1st floor+32* ▲ *Stalls,*
Escalator ▲ *1st floor+65* ▲ *Dress Circle*

Noel Coward

St Martin's Lane, WC2N 4AH
Box office: 0870 850 9919
Website: www.delfont-mackintosh.com
Tube: Leicester Square
Train: Charing Cross
Parking: Upper St Martin's Lane/Bedfordbury
❄ Air Condition   ◁ Infra-red
**⊙ Bridge at the rear links to Wyndhams so that if one theatre has a large
cast and there is spare room in the other actors can dress there.**

Actor manager Charles Wyndham built this theatre in 1903, as a larger
and grander companion to the existing theatre in Charing Cross Road
that still bears his name. Both theatres were designed by W G R Sprague
and sit back to back with similar French classical façades. The Albery's
auditorium has a Louis XVI inspired cream and gold decorative scheme,
with cameos on the side walls at circle levels and two gold angels representing Peace and Music attended by cupids illustrating Winter and Summer above the proscenium. It was originally known as the New Theatre
– Wyndham couldn't decide what to call it, so it was referred to as the new
theatre during construction, and the name stuck. Wyndham's successors
the Albery family renamed it after themselves in 1973, and in 2006 it became the Noel Coward. His first play *I'll Leave It To You* premiered here in
1920 - with Coward in the lead - although it only ran for five weeks. Its
role has generally been the home for star studded revivals of classic plays
and West End seasons by other producing companies. Wyndham and his
wife Mary Moore appeared in the opening production *Rosemary*. Among
the works to have premiered here were George Bernard Shaw's *St Joan*
(1924) with Sybil Thorndike, T S Eliot's *The Cocktail Party* (1950), and
Lionel Bart's *Oliver!* (1960) – its longest running success at 2618 performances. John Gielgud established himself as a star in *Hamlet* (1934) with the
second longest run of the play ever, and *Romeo And Juliet* (1935) in which
he and Laurence Olivier alternated the roles of Romeo and Mercutio.
From 1941 to 1950 the Sadler's Wells and Old Vic companies moved in to
present plays, opera and ballet, having lost their homes due to bomb damage. Productions included Ralph Richardson as *Peer Gynt* (1944), Olivier
and Richardson in *Uncle Vanya* (1946) and Edith Evans in *The Cherry Orchard* (1948). The new National Theatre company presented a season here
in 1971 with Laurence Olivier in *Long Day's Journey Into Night, Danton's
Death* and *Rules Of The Game*. More recently the Almeida Theatre made
The Albery their West End home with *Phèdre, Britannicus, Vassa* and *Plenty*
(1998-99). Recent productions include Lindsay Duncan and Alan Rickman in *Private Lives* (2001), Patrick Stewart in *The Master Builder* (2003)
and Michael Gambon and Lee Evans in *Endgame* (2004).

NOEL COWARD

Balcony

Grand Circle

Royal Circle

Stalls

Stage

55 ▲ *Balcony, 30* ▲ *Upper Circle, 3* ▲ *Dress Circle, 30* ▼ *Stalls, 3* ▲ *Foyer,* 🏛877

Novello

The Aldwych WC2B 5LD
Box office: 0870 950 0940
Website: www.delfont-mackintosh.com
Tube: Covent Garden/Holborn/Temple
Train: Charing Cross
Parking: Drury Lane/Bedfordbury
♿ *Dress Circle*
☉ *Putti cherubs above the boxes in the auditorium.*

It was designed by W G R Sprague as a twin to the Aldwych, bookending the block as he did later with the Gielgud/Queen's in Shaftesbury Avenue. This was the first to open in 1905 as the Waldorf Theatre, although it changed to the Strand in 1909, the Whitney in 1911, and back to the Strand in 1913. In 2005 it was reopened after an extensive refurbishment programme and renamed the Novello, in honour of the composer and actor Ivor Novello, who lived in a flat above the theatre for over thirty years. It has a classical facade in Portland stone with pediments and columns almost identical to the Aldwych, but with statues in front of the central columns on its top level. The interior in Louis XIV style is more lavish, with figures holding lamps at the foot of the staircase in the foyer leading to the auditorium, where the boxes are framed with marble Ionic pillars and surmounted by cupids. Above the proscenium is a bas-relief of Apollo in a chariot pulled by four horses, attended by goddesses and cupids, and on the ceiling there are allegorical figures painted after Le Brun. It received minor bomb damage in both World Wars, during performances by Fred Terry and Donald Wolfit respectively, which on neither occasion were abandoned. It opened with a programme alternating opera and plays in Italian with Elenora Duse and her company. Most of the great names of the time appeared here including, H B Irving in Lights Out (1905) and Herbert Beerbohm Tree in Oliver Twist (1905). It saw the British premiere of Chekhov's The Cherry Orchard (1909). Treasure Island was a regular Christmas visitor from 1922 to 1926. Mirroring the Aldwych farces came It's A Boy! (1930), It's A Girl! and Night Of The Garter (1932), 1066 And All That (1935), and then the Aldwych company moved in with Aren't Men Beasts (1936), A Spot Of Bother (1937), Banana Ridge (1938) and Spotted Dick (1939). Arsenic And Old Lace (1942) was its longest running show until Sailor Beware (1955) made a star of Peggy Mount; a record broken by the 11 year run of *No Sex Please - We're British!* (1971) which made a star of Michael Crawford. Important premiers in recent years include Tom Stoppard's The Real Thing (1982), David Mamet's A Life In The Theatre (1989) and Alan Ayckbourn's The Revenger's Comedies (1991). Since leaving the Barbican, the Royal Shakespeare Company has presented seasons of its Stratford productions here.

NOVELLO

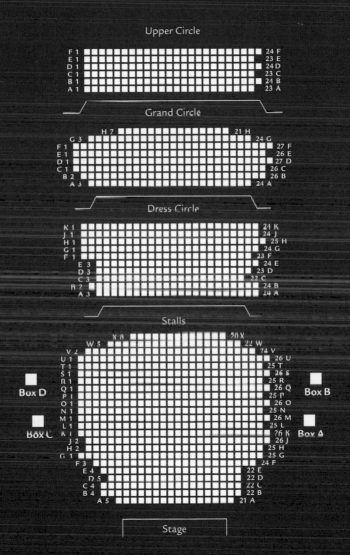

Upper Circle

F 1 ... 24 F
E 1 ... 23 E
D 1 ... 24 D
C 1 ... 23 C
B 1 ... 24 B
A 1 ... 23 A

Grand Circle

G 3 H 7 ... 21 H 24 G
F 1 ... 27 F
E 1 ... 26 E
D 1 ... 27 D
C 1 ... 26 C
B 2 ... 26 B
A 3 ... 24 A

Dress Circle

K 1 ... 24 K
J 1 ... 24 J
H 1 ... 25 H
G 1 ... 24 G
F 1 ... 23 F
E 3 ... 24 E
D 3 ... 24 D
C 3 ... 22 C
B ? ... 24 B
A 3 ... 24 A

Stalls

X 8 ... 20 X
W 5 ... 24 W
V 2 ... 24 V
U 1 ... 26 U
T 1 ... 25 T
S 1 ... 26 S
R 1 ... 25 R
Q 1 ... 26 Q
P 1 ... 25 P
O 1 ... 26 O
N 1 ... 25 N
M 1 ... 26 M
L 1 ... 25 L
K 1 ... 26 K
J 2 ... 26 J
H 2 ... 25 H
G 1 ... 25 G
F 3 ... 24 F
E 4 ... 22 E
D 5 ... 22 D
C 4 ... 22 C
B 4 ... 22 B
A 5 ... 21 A

Box D
Box B
Box C
Box A

Stage

70▲ Balcony, 40▲ Upper Circle, 7▲ Dress Circle, 32▼ Stalls
8▲ Foyer, ▥ 1067

99

The Old Vic

Waterloo Road SE1 8NB
Box office: 0870 060 6628
Website: www.oldvictheatre.com
Tube: Waterloo
Train: Waterloo
Parking: On street
 ♿ *Dress Circle*
❄ *Air Condition*
◉ *The auditorium retains the original ceiling, and the unusual barley sugar twist proscenium arch is surmounted by a coat of arms*

The Royal Coburg Theatre was designed by Rudolph Cabanel and opened in 1818. Unlicensed, it became a home for lurid melodramas, although Edmund Kean did appear there in 1831. A new management relaunched it as the Royal Victoria in 1833, but it sank even further, staging crude melodrama at very cheap prices. In 1858 sixteen people died and many were injured in a stampede, caused by a false alarm about a fire in the 'fourpenny gallery'. The building was partially reconstructed before opening as the New Victoria Palace music hall in 1871, again unsuccessfully. Emma Cons, a social reformer, took it over, and with the interior refurbished by J T Robinson, it reopened in 1881 as the Royal Victoria Hall and Coffee Tavern, presenting a programme of concerts, opera and scenes from Shakespeare. In 1912 the management passed to Cons's niece Lilian Baylis who had been acting manager since 1898. Despite having no previous experience, Baylis succeeded and went on to lay the foundations of many British cultural institutions. She began presenting full Shakespeare plays at popular prices, the Old Vic becoming the first theatre in the world to have completed the entire canon in 1923, with actors such as Peggy Ashcroft, Charles Laughton and Laurence Olivier. Seasons of opera and ballet were also introduced, and Baylis took over and rebuilt Sadler's Wells theatre in 1931. Circulating productions between the venues became too costly and inconvenient, especially when scenery blew off a lorry crossing Waterloo Bridge. Ballet and opera moved permanently to Sadler's Wells in 1935, later developing into the Royal Ballet and English National Opera. Drama continued after Baylis's death in 1937, moving to the West End after bomb damage and reopening in 1950. In 1963 the National Theatre Company took up residence and stayed until 1976. The Old Vic then fell on hard times and was often dark, until restored to it former glory by Ed Mirvish. Despite attempts to set up new companies by Jonathan Miller and Peter Hall it has failed to find a new role or continuing success. Kevin Spacey's appointment as artistic director in 2004 has met with equally mixed results.

The Old Vic

THE OLD VIC

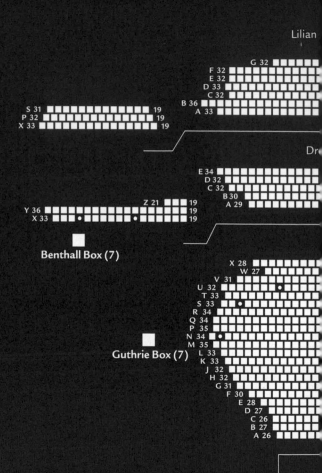

Lilian

Dr

G 32
F 32
E 32
D 33
C 32
B 36
A 33

S 31 — 19
P 32 — 19
X 33 — 19

E 34
D 32
C 32
B 30
A 29

Z 21 — 19
Y 36 — 19
X 33 — 19

Benthall Box (7)

X 28
W 27
V 31
U 32
T 33
S 33
R 34
Q 34
P 35
N 34
M 35
L 33
K 33
J 32
H 32
G 31
F 30
E 28
D 27
C 26
B 27
A 26

Guthrie Box (7)

Act I • The Old Vic

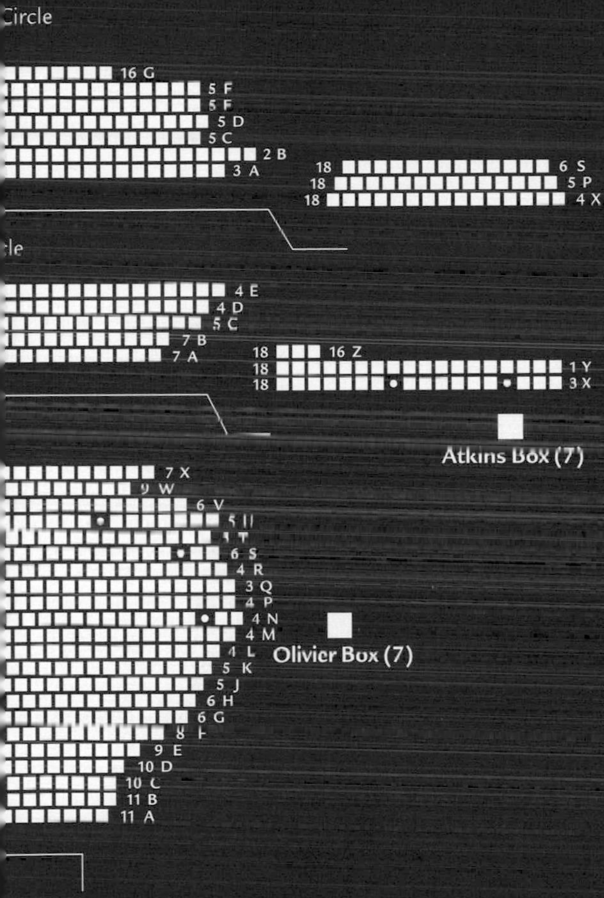

Circle

16 G
5 F
5 F
5 D
5 C
2 B
3 A

18   6 S
18   5 P
18   4 X

cle

4 E
4 D
5 C
7 B
7 A

18   16 Z
18   1 Y
18   3 X

Atkins Box (7)

7 X
9 W
6 V
5 U
4 T
6 S
4 R
3 Q
4 P
4 N
4 M
4 L   Olivier Box (7)
5 K
5 J
6 H
6 G
8 F
9 E
10 D
10 C
11 B
11 A

58▲ Upper Circle, 29▲ + 3▼ Dress Circle,
3▲ Stalls, 5▲ Foyer, 🔭 *1071*

Open Air

Inner Circle, Regent's Park, NW1 4NP
Box office: 0870 060 1811
Website: www.openairtheatre.org
Tube: Baker Street
Train: Marylebone
Parking: On street
⊰ FM Assisted Listening System ♿ Stalls
◉ *Performances from June to September with extra matinees to cater for school parties*

Open air productions of Shakespeare in Regent's Park were given by Ben Greet and his Woodland Players for a number of years from 1900 onwards. The idea was revived successfully in 1932, with performances of a 'black and white' production of *Twelfth Night* which had been running at the New Theatre. This resulted in a permanent open air theatre being set up in 1933 by Sydney Carroll and Robert Atkins, who continued to run it until 1960. A stage was built in front of existing trees, with shrubs planted at the sides to define it. The audience were seated in deck chairs on the facing slope with park benches at the rear. Lights and speakers were hung in trees. The programmes have mostly been Shakespeare, although Shaw's *The Six Of Calais* (1934) premiered here, and ballet and opera have also been presented. Among the actors who performed here in the early days were Gladys Cooper, Jack Hawkins, Deborah Kerr, Vivien Leigh, Anna Neagle and Jessica Tandy. In 1962 a new stage was built, and David Conville took over, forming the New Shakespeare Company which has been the resident company since. In 1976 the present stadium style building designed by Howell, Killick, Partridge and Amis was constructed, providing tip-up seating, with bar and food facilities beneath. This was extended by Haworth Tompkins in 2000 to provide enhanced technical and catering facilities. In recent years the season has developed into a pattern of two Shakespeares and a musical (particularly those with Shakespearean origin such as *The Boys From Syracuse* and *Kiss Me Kate*), plus a children's play presented in the mornings and afternoons. Unsurprisingly the most frequently performed play has been *A Midsummer Night's Dream*, the most regular Bottom being Robert Atkins, followed by the former Artistic Director Ian Talbot (also one of the great Toads in *Toad Of Toad Hall*). Other recent performers include Anthony Andrews, Michael Crawford, Ralph Fiennes, Edward Fox, Jeremy Irons, Felicity Kendal and Robert Stephens. Despite the vagaries of British weather, very few performances are actually cancelled each year. The time when stage lights take over as daylight fades is an experience of great theatrical magic not to be missed.

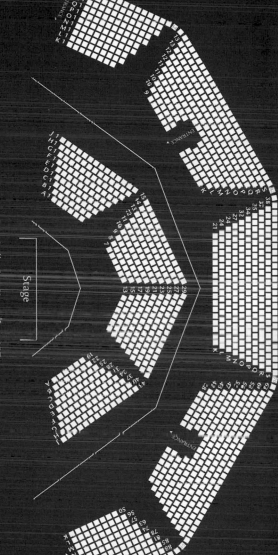

OPEN AIR

Stage

0► Stalls, 0► Foyer 🏛 187

Open Air Theatre

Palace

Cambridge Circus W1V 8AY
Box office: 0870 895 5579
Website: www.rutheatres.com
Tube: Leicester Square/Tottenham Court Road
Train: Charing Cross
Parking: Cambridge Circus/Wardour Street

✈ Infra-red ♿ Stalls

⊙ *Stalls Bar has an adjoining picture gallery with collection of photographs and drawings of past productions.*

Designed by T E Collcutt and G H Holloway under the supervision of impresario Richard D'Oyly Carte, and occupying a whole block, the Palace opened as the Royal English Opera House in 1891. The red brick and terracotta façade is in Renaissance style, with three bays containing groups of arcaded windows, friezes, statuary and domed octagonal towers to each side of the main frontage and was restored in 1989. Its commanding position makes it a London landmark. Inside the foyer, the grand staircase and Circle Bars are of marble. The long Stalls Bar of gilt, ornate plasterwork and mirrors remains in its original state. The stage was constructed to take the sliding scenery of the period and this also remains largely intact. It was intended to be the home of English opera, and opened with *Ivanhoe* by Arthur Sullivan and Julian Sturgis, but this was a complete flop, after which D'Oyly Carte tried French opera, and then Sarah Bernhardt as Cleopatra, equally unsuccessfully. Disillusioned, he sold out and it became the Palace Theatre of Varieties in 1892. Most of the great music hall artists of the time appeared here, and Pavlova made her London debut in 1910. Its peak as a music hall came with the staging of the first Royal Command Variety Performance in 1912, causing Oswald Stoll to comment "The Cinderella of the arts at last went to the Ball". Public interest moved on to revue and so came *The Passing Show* (1914), *Bric-à-Brac* (1915), *Vanity Fair* (1916) and *Airs And Graces* (1917). In the next craze it became a cinema. Live performance returned with the premieres of the musical comedies *No, No, Nanette* (1925), *The Girl Friend* (1927), *The Gay Divorcee* (1933), Cole Porter's *Anything Goes* (1935) and Rodgers and Hart's *On Your Toes* (1937). During World War II Jack Hulbert and Cecily Courtneidge starred in a succession of shows including *Under Your Hat* (1938) and *Something In The Air* (1943). In the 1950s the Palace was one of the theatres used by Peter Daubeny's World Theatre Seasons and it was also here that John Osbourne's *The Entertainer* (1957) starring Laurence Olivier transferred from the Royal Court. Its recent repertoire has included some of London's longest running shows *The Sound Of Music* (1961) and *Jesus Christ Superstar* (1972). *Les Miserables* (1985) which moved to the Queen's in 2004 after an 18 year run to be replaced by the *Monty Python's Spamalot*, which is still running.

PALACE

Balcony

Grand Circle

Dress Circle

Stalls

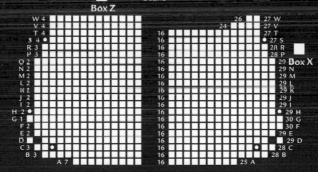

Stage

77▲ Balcony, 56▲ Upper Circle, 30▲ Dress Circle , 22▼ +18▲ Stalls
2▲ Foyer, ♿1400

Peacock

Portugal Street WC2A 2HT
Box office: 0870 737 0337
Website: www.sadlerswells.com
Tube: Covent Garden/Holborn/Temple
Train: Charing Cross
Parking: Drury Lane/On street
♿ *Dress Circle*
◉ *Dickens Old Curiosity Shop is located opposite the rear of the building*

The first theatre on this site, which opened in 1911 and occupied a whole block, was the London Opera House, conceived by American impresario Oscar Hammerstein as a rival to the Covent Garden. It was a grand building designed by Bertie Crewe with an interior of elegance and extravagance. Unfortunately for Hammerstein Covent Garden had the London rights to the most popular works, and the best known singers under contract, and he was forced to close. Seasons of variety, films, plays and pantomimes followed with little success. Oswald Stoll took it over and in 1917 renamed it the Stoll Picture Theatre with a successful formula combining a film with a resident Grand Orchestra featuring singers and instrumentalists. Live entertainment returned in 1941 with twice nightly variety and pantomime. After Stoll died in 1942 it became the Stoll Theatre, and presented revivals of *Lilac Time*, *Show Boat* and *The Student Prince*. In 1947 the stage was converted to an ice rink for a series of Ice Spectacles. The Festival Ballet, later to become English National Ballet, launched here successfully in 1951, and dance and opera seasons, interspersed with occasional musicals and transfers became the norm. The most successful were the Gershwins' *Porgy And Bess* (1952) and *Kismet* (1955). After a season by the Stratford Memorial Theatre of *Titus Andronicus* (1957) with Laurence Olivier and Vivien Leigh it closed and was sold for office development with the proviso that a theatre be included. In 1960 the current building opened as the Royalty Theatre, entirely underground and with the entrance moved to a side street. The interior was of contemporary design, and the stage had an adjustable proscenium arch to accommodate musicals or plays, but after a succession of short runs in 1961 it reverted to films. It returned to live shows with *Oh! Calcutta* (1970) its only real success, before becoming a television studio. When live shows returned in 1986 once again these were mostly short runs of opera and dance. In 1996 the London School of Economics took over the building for educational use, renaming it the Peacock Theatre. It is operated in partnership with Sadler's Wells which was based here while its own theatre was rebuilt, and continues to host British and international dance companies and Raymond Briggs's *The Snowman,* during the festive season.

PEACOCK

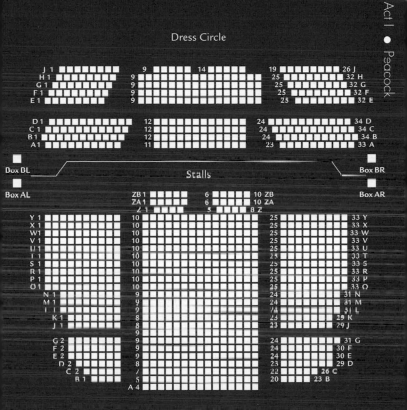

Dress Circle

Stalls

Phoenix

Charing Cross Road WC2H 0JP
Box office: 0870 060 6629
Website: www.theambassadors.com
Tube: Tottenham Court Road/Leicester Square
Train: Charing Cross
♿ Dress Circle Box
Parking: Cambridge Circus/Great Russell Street
◉ Foyer bar contains a display of Noel Coward memorabilia

In the 1920s this was the site of the Alcazar, a less than high class continuous variety house, whose novelty was three stages, with the audience moving from stage to stage between turns. The current building, which opened in 1930, was designed by the unique combination of Giles Gilbert Scott, Bertie Crewe, and Cecil Masey, with Theodore Komisarjevsky as art director. The exterior is an odd combination of classical stone entrances on two sides of the building, separated by an undistinguished brick block of shops and apartments. The original corner entrance in Charing Cross Road has a loggia with four columns above the canopy topped by an attic with square windows. The current entrance in Phoenix Street is a less formal two storey three bay arcade with twisted columns. Inside is an Art Deco gem of mirrored corridors and bars with painted ceilings. The auditorium has painted panels by Vladimir Polunin after Tintoretto, Titian and Giorgione above the boxes, and the entire safety curtain is a rendition of The Triumph Of Love. Famous actors in well-made plays have provided the Phoenix's staple fare. The opening production was the premiere of Noel Coward's *Private Lives* with Coward, Gertrude Lawrence, Adrianne Allen and Laurence Olivier. This was followed by a succession of flops and a resort to variety, before Coward and Lawrence returned with *Tonight At 8.30* (1936). After this success was again lacking and films were shown in 1938. The first real hit was Cicely Courtneidge in *Under The Counter* (1945). Terrence Rattigan's double bill of *The Browning Version* and *Harlequinade* (1948) fared better than *The Sleeping Prince* (1953) with Laurence Olivier and Vivien Leigh. Other plays to premiere here were Thornton Wilder's *The Skin Of Our Teeth* (1945) with Vivien Leigh, Arthur Miller's *Death Of A Salesman* (1949), John Van Druten's *Bell, Book And Candle* (1954), Tom Stoppard's biggest commercial success *Night And Day* (1978), and Sondheim's *Into The Woods* (1990). In 1976 a Hollywood season saw Rock Hudson and Juliet Prowse in *I Do I Do*, Glynis Johns and Louis Jourdan in *13, Rue De L'Amour*, Lee Remmick in *Bus Stop* and Douglas Fairbanks in *The Pleasure Of His Company*. The unlikely musical *The Canterbury Tales* (1968) proved to be its longest running production. *Blood Brothers* has been here ever since and is the 5th longest running show in West End history..

PHOENIX

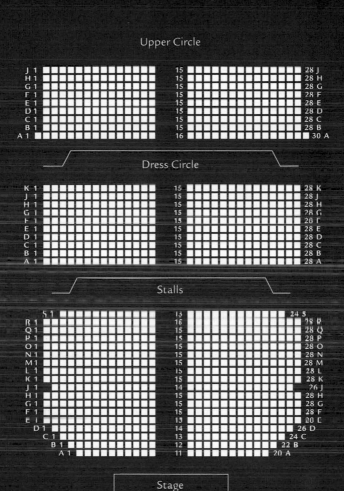

Upper Circle

J 1		15	28 J
H 1		15	28 H
G 1		15	28 G
F 1		15	28 F
E 1		15	28 E
D 1		15	28 D
C 1		15	28 C
B 1		15	28 B
A 1		16	30 A

Dress Circle

K 1		15	28 K
J 1		15	28 J
H 1		15	28 H
G 1		15	28 G
F 1		15	20 F
E 1		15	28 E
D 1		15	28 D
C 1		15	28 C
B 1		15	28 B
A 1		15	28 A

Stalls

S 1		13	24 S
R 1		16	28 R
Q 1		15	28 Q
P 1		15	28 P
O 1		15	28 O
N 1		15	28 N
M 1		15	28 M
L 1		15	28 L
K 1		15	28 K
J 1		14	26 J
H 1		15	28 H
G 1		15	28 G
F 1		15	28 F
E 1		13	20 E
D 1		14	26 D
C 1		13	24 C
B 1		12	22 B
A 1		11	20 A

Stage

Piccadilly

Denman Street, W1V 8DY
Box office: 0870 060 6641
Website: www.theambassadors.com
Tube: Piccadilly Circus
Train: Charing Cross
Parking: Denman Street/Brewer Street

♿ Dress Circle

✮ Air Condition

◉ *A false ceiling was installed which could be lowered to reduce the seating capacity by cutting off the Upper Circle*

Built on the site of former stables, the Piccadilly was designed by Bertie Crewe in conjunction with Edward A Stone, and opened in 1928. The curved exterior of the corner site, looking like stone but actually white cement, echoes the classically influenced Nash buildings in Regent Street. The interior was designed in Art Deco style by French designers Marc-Henri Levy and Gaston Laverdet, but this was replaced by a generic classical scheme in 1955. It has had a troubled history, embracing musicals (many of which flopped) classic drama, and dark periods. After opening with Evelyn Laye in Jerome Kern's *Blue Eyes* it soon succumbed to cinema, showing the first talking picture to be seen in Britain: *Singing Fool* with Al Jolson. Live shows returned but not very successfully, and in 1937 a new format called *Choose Your Time* was launched, with a continuous programme consisting of newsreel, 'swingphonic orchestra', individual acts, cartoon and a short comedy play. This fared no better, and transfers of long running shows at reduced prices became the norm until the premiere of Noel Coward's *Blithe Spirit* (1941) – but this soon transferred elsewhere. John Gielgud's *Macbeth* (1942) lived up to the play's unlucky reputation with four of the cast dying and the designer committing suicide; shortly afterwards the building suffered bomb damage and closed. On reopening Noel Coward's revue *Sigh No More* (1945) was followed by *Antony And Cleopatra* (1946), then it was back to transfers. Successes came with the London premieres of Broadway hits, Edward Albee's *Who's Afraid Of Virginia Woolf?* (1964), *Man Of La Mancha* (1968 and 1969), Angela Lansbury in *Gypsy* (1973), Claire Bloom in Tennessee Williams's *A Streetcar Named Desire* (1974) and Henry Fonda as *Clarence Darrow* (1975). In 1980 the Royal Shakespeare Company production of Willy Russell's *Educating Rita* launched the career of Julie Walters. A series of megamusical flops followed with *Mutiny* (1985), *Metropolis* (1989), *King* (1990), and *Which Witch* (1992). It was redeemed by the longest ever West End run of a ballet with Matthew Bourne's *Swan Lake* (1996) and revivals of *Noises Off* (2001) and *Guys And Dolls* (2005). Piccadilly is soon to be the venue for a stage version of *Grease*, with stars chosen by the audience of an ITV talent show.

PICCADILLY

Upper Circle

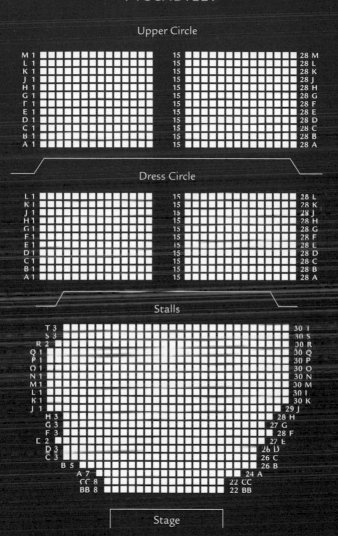

M 1	15	28 M
L 1	15	28 L
K 1	15	28 K
J 1	15	28 J
H 1	15	28 H
G 1	15	28 G
F 1	15	28 F
E 1	15	28 E
D 1	15	28 D
C 1	15	28 C
B 1	15	28 B
A 1	15	28 A

Dress Circle

L 1	15	28 L
K 1	15	28 K
J 1	15	28 J
H 1	15	28 H
G 1	15	28 G
F 1	15	28 F
E 1	15	28 E
D 1	15	28 D
C 1	15	28 C
B 1	15	28 B
A 1	15	28 A

Stalls

T 3		30 T
S 3		30 S
R 2		30 R
Q 1		30 Q
P 1		30 P
O 1		30 O
N 1		30 N
M 1		30 M
L 1		30 L
K 1		30 K
J 1		29 J
H 3		28 H
G 3		27 G
F 3		28 F
E 2		27 E
D 3		26 D
C 3		26 C
B 5		26 B
A 7		24 A
CC 8		22 CC
BB 8		22 BB

Stage

70 ▲ Upper Circle, 6 ▲ Dress Circle, 15 ▼ Stalls, 1 ▲ Foyer, 🔊 1,213

115

Playhouse

Northumberland Avenue WC2N 5DE
Box office: 0870 060 6631
Website: www.theambassadors.com
Tube: Embankment/Charing Cross
Train: Charing Cross
Parking: Trafalgar Square/Limited on street
✳ *Air Condition*   ⊲ *Infra-red*
☉ *The safety curtain is painted in the style of the original act drop*

Rumour has it that the first theatre on this site, the Royal Avenue (1882), was built because its owner Sefton Parry believed that the South Eastern Railway Company would want to acquire it for an extension to Charing Cross Station, at great profit to himself. He was wrong. It opened with a French comic opera *Madame Favart*, which was followed by more of the same, but a change of policy brought drama with the first plays of George Bernard Shaw, *Arms And The Man* (1894), and Somerset Maugham, *A Man Of Honour* (1901). The reconstruction of the theatre to a second design by the original architect F H Fowler was almost completed in 1905, when part of the station collapsed onto the site, killing six people, injuring twenty six, and badly damaging the theatre. When compensation of £20,000 was finally received the current theatre was constructed. A new design by Detmar Blow and Fernand Billerey, retaining most of the exterior but with a new interior, opened in 1907 as the Playhouse. The façade is of Portland stone in French Renaissance style. The auditorium in Franco-Venetian style has fine plasterwork, upper boxes supported by statuary and with ornamental lamppost light fittings, and balustraded circle fronts. Gladys Cooper, one of the few female actor managers, starred with Gerald du Maurier in many of the plays she produced here, which included *White Cargo* (1924) and *The Painted Veil* (1931), and the premiere of Maugham's *Home And Beauty* (1919). Apart from seasons by Nancy Price's People's National Theatre (1938-39) and the Old Vic, when Peter Ustinov's early play *Blow Your Own Trumpet* was shown, it was mostly short runs – one revue lasted only two nights – and dark periods. In 1951 the BBC took it over and many radio comedy programmes, such as *Hancock's Half Hour* and *The Goon Show*, and panel games were recorded here over the next twenty five years. Music programmes, some of which featured early appearances by The Beatles and The Rolling Stones, were also produced here. Abandoned for ten years, the Playhouse was restored and reopened in 1987, but a succession of managements, including a Peter Hall Company season of Tennessee Williams's *The Rose Tattoo*, *Twelfth Night* and Molière's *Tartuffe* and *A Doll's House* (1996) have failed to break the short run/dark spell cycle.

PLAYHOUSE

Upper Circle

Dress Circle

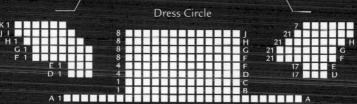

Stalls

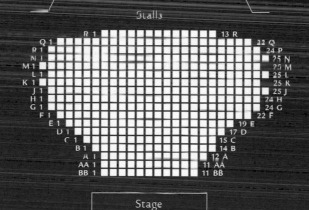

Stage

88 ▲ Upper Circle, 29 ▲ Dress Circle, 0 ▲ Stalls, 3 ▲ Foyer, ♿ 756

117

Prince Edward

Old Compton Street, W1V 6HS
Box office: 0870 850 9191
Website: www.delfont-mackintosh.com
Tube: Leicester Square/Tottenham Court Road
Train: Charing Cross
Parking: Cambridge Circus/Wardour Street
♿ *Dress Circle/ Royal Box*
✨ *Air Condition* ⏜ *Infra-red*
◉ *Unusual circular foyer and stepped loges at the sides of the auditorium*

Built on the site of The Emporium, a former royal draper's shop, the Prince Edward was designed by Edward A Stone, with an interior by French designers Marc-Henri Levy and Gaston Laverdet and opened in 1930. The red brick exterior is in the style of an Italian palazzo, incorporating a loggia colonnade at first floor level, whose windows were originally fitted with green shutters. The Art Deco auditorium with rectilinear patterns made use of a new material Marb-L-Cote, and the proscenium was framed in amber Rene Lalique glass – no longer extant. It opened with the show *Rio Rita (1930)*, but despite trying musicals, cabaret with *Josephine Baker* (1933), non-stop revue, talkies and trade shows the theatre was not successful. It was reconstructed by Stone into a cabaret-restaurant with a dance floor, staircases from the stalls to the dress circle and stepped loges at the sides, reopening in 1936 as the London Casino. With lavish shows such as *Folies Parisiennes* it soon became the most profitable entertainment venue in London taking £7000 a week. Having closed during the Blitz in 1940, it re-emerged as the Queensbury All Services Club in 1942 with on-stage seating round a boxing ring, and remained as such until the end of World War II. Theatre returned with *Pick Up Girl* (1946), *The Dancing Years* (1947), variety, ballet seasons and pantomime. In 1949 Robert Nesbitt's *Latin Quarter* cabaret show was staged and ran on into several editions. In 1954 Cinerama arrived in London with a huge semicircular screen installed on the stage. When this fad was over it remained as a cinema showing long runs including *How The West Was Won* (1962) and *2001: A Space Odyssey* (1968). In 1974 a mixed programme of pantomime, live shows and films was launched with *Cinderella* starring Twiggy, but most shows were flops. Its fortunes changed in 1978 when it reverted to the original name of Prince Edward with Tim Rice and Andrew Lloyd Webber's *Evita*. Since then it has seen a succession of long running musicals; *Chess* (1986), *Anything Goes* (1989), *Crazy For You* (1993), *Mamma Mia!* (2000), and *Mary Poppins* (2004) interspersed with the continually reworked *Martin Guerre* (1996). A refurbishment in 1992 restored the theatre to something approaching its original design scheme.

Prince Edward

Grand Circle

Dress Circle

Stalls

Stage

41 ▲ Upper Circle, 13 ▲ Dress Circle, 22 ▼ Stalls, 0 ▲ Foyer, 🏛 1622

Prince Edward

Prince of Wales

Coventry Street, W1V 8AS
Box office: 0870 850 0393
Website: www.delfont-mackintosh.com
Tube: Piccadilly Circus/Leicester Square
Train: Charing Cross
Parking: Whitcomb Street/Denman Street
✳ *Air Condition* ⤙ *Infra-red*
◉ *Stalls Bar has an extensive collection of posters from previous productions*

The first theatre on the site was designed by C J Phipps in Moorish style, and opened in 1884 as the Prince's. It was renamed the Prince Of Wales in 1886 when another theatre of that name closed and became a Salvation Army hostel. The current building, which was designed by Robert Cromie in restrained Art Deco style, opened in 1937. The exterior is in artificial stone with a commanding circular tower above its corner entrance. The wide and shallow auditorium is on just two levels, with the Circle front only 21 feet from the pit rail. It was extensively refurbished in 2004 in lavish Art Deco style exceeding that of the original design scheme. The large bar beneath the Stalls, now called the Delfont Room, stages occasional cabaret performances. It has been notable for introducing a number of theatrical ideas to London. *L'Enfant Prodigue* (1891) 'a wordless play' with mimes led to the establishment of the first British Pierrot troupe. *In Town* (1892) described as a 'musical farce' was a prototype musical comedy, and its success spawned others including *A Gaiety Girl* (1893), *Gentleman Joe* (1895), *The School Girl* (1903) and *Lady Madcap* (1904). The famous André Charlot revues *Bran Pie* (1919), *A to Z* (1921), *Charlot's Revue* (1924) and *Charlot's Show* (1926) featured Gertrude Lawrence, Beatrice Lillie, Jessie Matthews and Jack Buchanan. These were followed by less prestigious non-stop revue until the theatre closed in 1937. The new building opened with *Les Folies de Paris et Londres*, and continued with similar shows. *Strike A New Note* (1943) brought comedian Sid Field to the West End; he also starred in *Strike It Again* (1944), *Piccadilly Hayride* (1946), and *Harvey* (1949). Mae West appeared in *Diamond Lil* (1948). The 1950s saw a succession of variety spectaculars with Frankie Howerd, Norman Wisdom, Benny Hill, Max Bygraves and others. It then became home to American shows *The World Of Suzie Wong* (1959), Neil Simon's *Come Blow Your Horn* (1962), Barbra Streisand in *Funny Girl* (1962), *Sweet Charity* (1967), and *Promises Promises* (1969). Recent years have seen a mixture of new and revived musicals including *Underneath The Arches* (1982), *Annie Get Your Gun* (1992), and *West Side Story* (1999). The programme of popular musicals has continued into the new century with *Fosse* (2000), *The Full Monty* (2002) and the transfer of *Mamma Mia!* (2004).

Circle

Stalls

Sound Desk

Circle Box 1
1 2 3 4

Circle Box 3
1 2 3 4

Circle Box 2
1 2 3 4

Circle Box 4
1 2 3 4

Stage

41 ▲ Upper Circle, 13 ▲ Dress Circle, 22 ▼ Stalls, 0 ▲ Foyer, 1622

Queen's

Shaftesbury Avenue, W1V 8BA
Box office: 0870 950 0930
Website: www.delfont-mackintosh.com
Tube: Piccadilly Circus
Train: Charing Cross
Parking: Brewer Street/Wardour Street

& Dress Circle

✻ Air Condition   ◁ Infra-red

⊙ Photographs of the original Sprague façade and foyer can be found in the lobby

This W G R Sprague designed theatre opened in 1907 and, like his Novello and Aldwych theatres, it bookends a whole block with the Gielgud Theatre. The two theatres were originally very similar, with Queen's being the slightly larger and more imposing of the two. It suffered severe bomb damage in 1940 and remained closed until 1959. A dull contemporary exterior and front of house was designed by Bryan Westwood and Hugh Casson, while the auditorium was restored to something approaching its original form. This is in similar grand Louis XVI style to the Gielgud, in red, white and gold, including a domed ceiling with elaborate plasterwork. The opening show was a flop and various managements tried their hand, including H B Irving producing and starring in some of his father Henry's successes, *The Bells*, *Louis XI* and *Hamlet* (1909-11). In 1913 'Tango Teas' were introduced, with the stalls transformed into a dance floor with tables surrounding it. The first success was two American comedians in *Potash And Perlmutter* (1914) and its sequel *Potash And Perlmutter In Society* (1916). The 1930s saw a succession of quality productions with Shaw's *The Apple Cart* (1929), the Old Vic production of John Gielgud's *Hamlet*, *The Barratts Of Wimpole Street*, *The Farmer's Wife*, Shaw's *Heartbreak House*, and Robert Morley's first play *Short Story* (1935). There was a Gielgud season (1937) in which he not only starred in *Richard II, The Merchant Of Venice, The Three Sisters* and *The School For Scandal*, but also directed the first two. It reopened in 1959 with Gielgud's Shakespeare recital *The Ages Of Man*. Noel Coward made his final West End appearance here in 1966. Shows which premiered here since include Anthony Newley's *Stop The World I Want To Get Off* (1961), Joe Orton's *What The Butler Saw* (1969), Tom Courtenay in *The Dresser* (1980), Julian Mitchell's *Another Country* (1982) and Stephen Sondheim's *Passion* (1996). *Les Miserables* transferred here in 2004 and is now London's longest running musical and the second longest running West End show after *The Mousetrap*. Following the recent acquisition of the Queen's and Gielgud by Cameron Mackintosh, major building works are being undertaken including the addition of a new theatre (called the Sondheim) above the Queen's.

QUEEN'S

Upper Circle

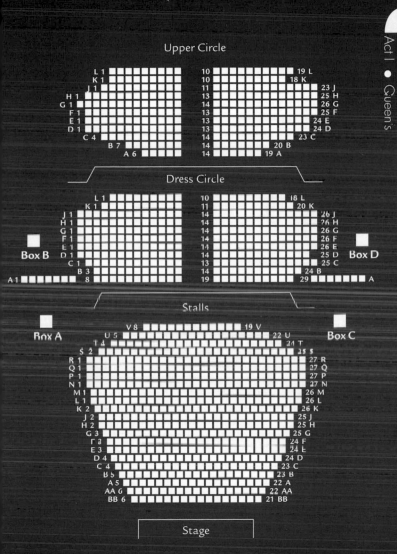

L 1 | 10 | 19 L
K 1 | 10 | 18 K
J 1 | 11 | 23 J
H 1 | 13 | 25 H
G 1 | 14 | 26 G
F 1 | 13 | 25 F
E 1 | 13 | 24 E
D 1 | 13 | 24 D
C 4 | 14 | 23 C
B 7 | 14 | 20 B
A 6 | 14 | 19 A

Dress Circle

L 1 | 10 | 18 L
K 1 | 11 | 20 K
J 1 | 14 | 26 J
H 1 | 14 | 26 H
G 1 | 14 | 26 G
F 1 | 14 | 26 F
E 1 | 14 | 26 E
D 1 | 14 | 25 D
C 1 | 13 | 25 C
B 3 | 14 | 24 B
A 1 | 8 | 19 | 29 | A

Box B   Box D

Stalls

Box A   Box C

V 8 | 19 V
U 5 | 22 U
T 4 | 24 T
S 2 | 25 S
R 1 | 27 R
Q 1 | 27 Q
P 1 | 27 P
N 1 | 27 N
M 1 | 26 M
L 1 | 26 L
K 2 | 26 K
J 2 | 25 J
H 2 | 25 H
G 3 | 25 G
F 3 | 24 F
E 3 | 24 E
D 4 | 24 D
C 4 | 23 C
B 5 | 23 B
A 5 | 22 A
AA 6 | 22 AA
BB 6 | 21 BB

Stage

39▲ Upper Circle, 18▲ Dress Circle, 21▼ Stalls, 1▲ Foyer, 🎭 *977*

125

Royal Court

Sloane Square, SW1W 8AS
Box office: 020 7565 5000
Website: www.royalcourttheatre.com
Tube: Sloane Square
Train: Victoria
Parking: Semley Place/Warwick Way
   ♿ *Dress Circle* ✻ *Air Condition* ◁ *Infra-red*
   ☉ *Restaurant, bookshop, and bar open all day*

Sloane Square had a theatre on its south side from 1870, when a disused chapel was converted into the New Chelsea, which then became the Belgravia. This was reconstructed as the Royal Court in 1871 and staged the premieres of Arthur Wing Pinero's farces. When redevelopment required its demolition, the present building, designed by Walter Emden and Bertie Crewe, was constructed as a replacement on the east side of the Square, opening in 1888. The exterior is of stone and red brick in Italian Renaissance style and the interior has undergone several reconstructions. After bomb damage it was remodelled by Robert Cromie in 1952, when the Gallery was shut off and converted into offices, and the rehearsal room at the top of the building was turned into a restaurant. This became the Theatre Upstairs studio theatre in 1971. The building underwent major refurbishment in 2000 by Haworth Tompkins, whose decorative style was to remove the plasterwork and not replace it. The Royal Court enjoyed its first great age under Harley Granville-Barker and J E Vedrenne (1904-07), when 32 plays were presented. Of these 11 were by Shaw including *Man And Superman* and *Major Barbara*, plus Galsworthy's *The Silver Box*, and Elizabeth Robins' *Votes For Women*. Shaw returned with *Heartbreak House* (1921) and *Back To Methuselah* (1924). The theatre's second golden age dawned in 1956 when the English Stage Company under George Devine took over, dedicated to producing new writing. It was immediately successful, changing the course of British drama with productions such as John Osborne's *Look Back In Anger* (1956) and *The Entertainer* (1957) with Laurence Olivier. Other writers performed here include John Arden, Christopher Hampton, David Hare and Caryl Churchill. It has also presented contemporary European writers, including Beckett, Brecht and Sartre, and continues to be the 'national theatre of new writing'. Recent discoveries have been Terry Johnson's *Hysteria* (1993), Kevin Elyot's *My Night With Reg* (1994), Sarah Kane's *Blasted* (1996), Mark Ravenhill's *Shopping And Fucking* (1996) and Conor McPherson's *The Weir* (1997). In 2007 Dominic Cooke was appointed the theatre's Artistic Director, following in the illustrious footsteps of Ian Rickson, Stephen Daldry and Max Stafford-Clark.

JERWOOD THEATRE DOWNSTAIRS

Act I • Royal Court

Balcony

Box B   C 1 ▢▢▢...21 C   Box D
         B 1 ▢▢▢...22 B
         A 1 ▢▢▢...21 A

Circle

Slips   Slips
11   12
10   E 3 ▢▢▢...20 E   13
9   D 2 ▢▢▢...20 D   14
8   C 2 ▢▢▢...21 C   15
Box A 7 B 1 ▢▢▢...21 B Box C 16
6   A 3 ▢▢▢...20 A   17
5   18
4   19

Stalls

         M 7 ▢▢▢...16 M
      L 6 ▢▢▢ 12 ▢▢ 17 L
      K 4 ▢▢▢ 12 ▢▢ 19 K

      J 3 ▢▢▢...20 J
      H 4 ▢▢▢...20 H
      G 3 ▢▢▢...20 G
      F 2 ▢▢▢...20 F
      E 3 ▢▢▢...20 E
      D 3 ▢▢▢...19 D
      C 4 ▢▢▢...19 C
      B 4 ▢▢▢...18 B
      A 5 ▢▢▢...18 A
     BB 6 ▢▢▢...16 BB
     AA 7 ▢▢▢...16 AA

Also:
Jerwood Theatre Upstairs
 ♿ Stalls Lift available
▲ 64 Stalls Lift available
🚻 77

39▲ Upper Circle, 18▲ Dress Circle, 21▼ Stalls, 1▲ Foyer, 🚻 977

127

Royal Opera House

Bow Street, Covent Garden, WC2E 9DD
Box office: 020 7304 4000
Website: www.royalopera.org
Tube: Covent Garden/Holborn/Temple
Train: Charing Cross
Parking: Drury Lane/Shelton Street
♿ *Stalls*

✱ *Air Condition*   ❮ *Infra-red*

◉ *Floral Hall foyer bar, restaurant and bookshop open all day.*

The first theatre on this site was constructed in 1732 to house a company holding the second Royal Patent allowing it to perform plays. Among early premieres were Handel's *Alcina* (1735), *Atalanta* (1736) and *Berenice* (1737), possibly the first public performance of a piano (1767), Oliver Goldsmith's *She Stoops To Conquer* (1773), Richard Brinsley Sheridan's *The Rivals* (1775), the pantomime *Aladdin* (1788), and the first melodrama *A Tale Of Mystery* (1802). William Betty, a thirteen year old 'child tragedian' became the rage in 1804 playing major Shakespearean roles including Hamlet. A fire destroyed the building along with Handel's organ and many scores in 1808. When the second theatre opened the following year an attempt was made to raise the prices, provoking the Old Price Riots, which resulted in the Riot Act being read from the stage and, ultimately, an apology from the management. William Charles Macready revolutionised stage illumination here in 1837 with the introduction of limelight. After considerable interior alterations, the theatre became The Royal Italian Opera in 1847. The current building, designed by Edward M Barry, in Roman Renaissance style with a Corinthian portico incorporating some statuary and bas-reliefs from the previous theatre, opened in 1858. The interior is majestic with a Grand Staircase rising between allegorical paintings to the Crush Bar, a great hall with 20ft high paintings and chandelier. The cream, gold and red auditorium includes a scene of Orpheus playing a lyre above the proscenium. Apart from an earlier conversion from boxes to open seating in the circle levels and a recent re-raking of the stalls to improve sightlines the auditorium remains substantially the same today. It dropped the "Italian" to become the Royal Opera House in 1892. After the Second World War, during which the building was converted into a Mecca dance hall, new management was put in place. The Sadler's Wells Ballet was invited to become the resident ballet company, re-opening the Royal Opera House with a performance of *Sleeping Beauty* in 1946, and the Covent Garden Opera Company was established as the resident opera company in the same year. These companies were to become, respectively, the Royal Ballet (1956) and the Royal Opera (1968), which have co-existed at the venue ever since.. The Linbury enables the company to perform small scale and experimental work, recitals, and show productions by outside companies.

128

Royal Opera House

ROYAL OPERA HOUSE

COVENT GARDEN

ROYAL OPERA HOUSE

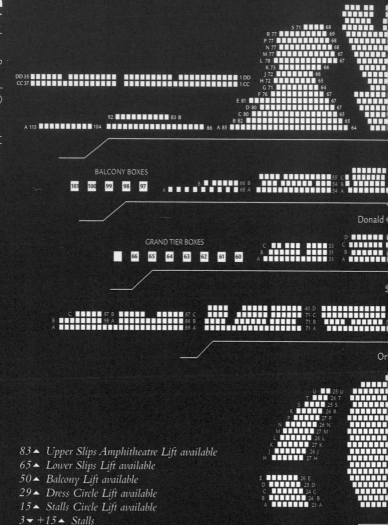

BALCONY BOXES

GRAND TIER BOXES

Donald

Or

83▲ Upper Slips Amphitheatre Lift available
65▲ Lower Slips Lift available
50▲ Balcony Lift available
29▲ Dress Circle Lift available
15▲ Stalls Circle Lift available
3▼ +15▲ Stalls
0▲ Foyer, ♿ 2260

130

51
49
55 47
54 47
47
48
48
49
50
49 50
51
51
48
49
50
50
51
51

38 S
38 R
37 P
37 N
37 M
37 L
41 K
43 J
43 H
43 G
38 F

BB 1   21   35 BB
AA 1   22   37 AA

34 E
36 D
34 C
33 B   B 10   1 B
29 A   11 A   1 A

and Tier

34 D   30 D
32 C   20 C
13 B   27 R
35 A   19 A   16 B
                            10 A   DALCONY BOXES
                            71 70 69 68 67

13 U
12 C   3 C
13 B   3 B   43 42 41 40 39 38 37 36
13 A   1 A

16 D   1 D
43 C   17 C   17 A
43 B   16 B   1 B
43 A   15 A   7 A   1 A

alls

3 W
10 V
7 U   5 U
7 T   4 T
7 S   3 S
7 R   2 R
7 R   1 R
7 N   1 N
7 M   1 M
7 L   1 L
7 K   1 K
7 J   1 J
7 H   1 H
7 G   1 G
7 F   1 F
7 E   1 E
7 D   1 D
7 C   1 C
8 B   1 B
8 A   1 A

Linbury Studio
& Stalls
27▼ Dress Circle Lift available
🔭 420

131

Shaftesbury

Shaftesbury Avenue, WC2H 8DP
Box office: 020 7379 5399
Website: www.shaftesbury-theatre.com
Tube: Tottenham Court Road/Holborn/Covent Garden
Train: Charing Cross
Parking: Museum Street/Drury Lane
  ⟁ *Box*
  ✱ *Air Condition*   ⤙ *Infra-red*
  ◉ *Dress Circle bar is in a Jacobean style with oak panelling and wrought iron.*

The Theatre now known as the Shaftesbury opened in 1911 as the New Prince's Theatre, dropping the New in 1914, before assuming its current title in 1963. Designed by Bertie Crew, its stone exterior is Modern Renaissance style with a tower above the corner entrance. The auditorium is considered to be one of the most beautiful in London, with French wedding cake style plasterwork in pink and white. Seated life-size classical figures, representing Comedy, Tragedy, Poetry and Music, surmount the boxes, which are supported by Ionic columns. Conceived as a home for melodrama at popular prices, its intimate feel coupled with a large seating capacity makes it suitable for everything from drama to opera and ballet. From the start its fare was eclectic, encompassing romantic opera such as *Monsieur Beaucaire* (1919), Sarah Bernhardt's final London performance as *Daniel* (1921), Diaghilev's Russian Ballet (1921 and 1927), *Macbeth* with Sybil Thorndyke (1926) and *Funny Face* with Fred and Adele Astaire (1928). At various points in its history, the Shaftesbury has provided a temporary venue for other theatres' companies – the D'Oyly Carte Opera company performed here in 1919, Sadler's Wells opera and ballet in 1944, and it was one of the theatres used by the Royal Opera when Covent Garden was closed in 1998. Since World War II it has mostly been home to musicals with *Pal Joey* (1954), *Wonderful Town* (1955), *How To Succeed In Business Without Really Trying* (1963), Lionel Bart's notorious flop *Twang!* (1965), *Follies* (1987), *Kiss Of The Spider Woman* (1992), *Carousel* (1993), *Tommy* (1996), *Rent* (1998) and *Thoroughly Modern Millie* (2003). The most controversial was *Hair* (1968) 'the tribal love rock musical' which delayed its opening until the day after the abolition of theatre censorship, and made good use of it by bringing nudity to the London stage. In 1973 just short of its 2000th performance part of the auditorium ceiling collapsed bringing an end to the run, and many people thought the theatre, but it was eventually listed, repaired and reopened in 1974. In 1984 The Theatre Of Comedy Company acquired it and staged a mixture of new works and classics including *See How They Run* (1984), *Pygmalion* (1984) and *An Italian Straw Hat* (1986).

138

SHAFTESBURY

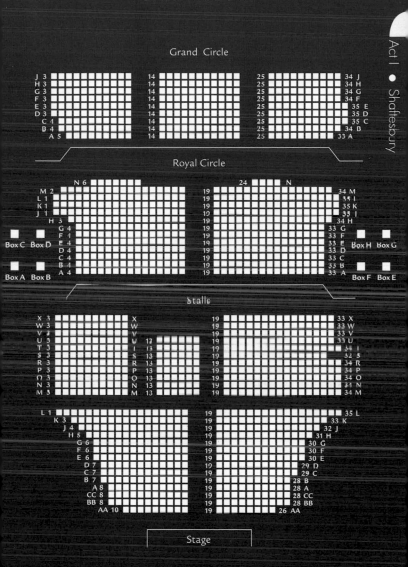

Grand Circle

J 3	14	25	34 J
H 3	14	25	34 H
G 3	14	25	34 G
F 3	14	25	34 F
E 3	14	25	35 E
D 3	14	25	35 D
C 4	14	25	35 C
B 4	14	25	34 B
A 5	14	25	33 A

Royal Circle

N 6   24   N

M 2	19	34 M
L 1	19	35 L
K 1	19	35 K
J 1	19	35 J
H 3	19	34 H
G 4	19	33 G
F 4	19	33 F
E 4	19	33 E
D 4	19	33 D
C 4	19	33 C
B 4	19	33 B
A 4	19	33 A

Box C   Box D   Box H   Box G

Box A   Box B   Box F   Box E

Stalls

X 3	X	19	33 X
W 3	W	19	33 W
V 3	V	19	33 V
U 3	U	12	19	33 U
T 3	T	13	19	34 T
S 3	S	13	19	32 S
R 3	R	13	19	34 R
P 3	P	13	19	34 P
O 3	O	13	19	34 O
N 3	N	13	19	34 N
M 3	M	13	19	34 M

L 1	19	35 L
K 3	19	33 K
J 4	19	32 J
H 5	19	31 H
G 6	19	30 G
F 6	19	30 F
E 6	19	30 E
D 7	19	29 D
C 7	19	29 C
B 7	19	28 B
A 8	19	28 A
CC 8	19	28 CC
BB 8	19	28 BB
AA 10	19	26 AA

Stage

60▲ Upper Circle, 0▲ Dress Circle, 22▼ Stalls, 1▲ Foyer, 🏛 *1408*

139

Shakespeare's Globe

New Globe Walk, SE1 9DT
Box office: 020 7401 9919
Website: www.shakespeares-globe.org
Tube: London Bridge/Southwark/Blackfriars
Train: London Bridge/Blackfriars
Parking: Upper Thames Street/On street
♿ Yard ❊ Induction Loop

◉ *Performances May to September but exhibition, restaurant and bookshop open all year round*

The first public playhouse in London was The Theatre, constructed outside the city wall to the north in Shoreditch in 1576, and managed by the actor James Burbage. It was in the form now familiar to us through the film Shakespeare In Love, with half the audience standing in the open air yard below the stage and the rest seated under cover in three shallow galleries surrounding them. The Theatre was so successful that Burbage built another, The Curtain, nearby the following year. A rival company run by Philip Henslowe built The Rose in 1587 on the south side of the river in Bankside. This was a rough area famous for entertainments such as cock fighting, bear baiting and bare knuckle boxing matches. In 1594 The Swan was built by Francis Langley at the west end of Bankside. By this time each of the theatres had a resident dramatist. Shakespeare arrived in London in the 1580s and began to work at The Theatre. When James Burbage died in 1597 his sons Richard and Cuthbert were unable to renew the lease on the land where The Theatre stood. Their response was to dismantle the building, transport it across the river and erect it in Bankside near the others, and rechristen it The Globe. Its first recorded performance was *Julius Caesar* on 21st September 1599 and it became the most famous of London's theatres, presenting Shakespeare's plays, with Richard Burbage creating many of the leading roles. In 1613 during a performance of *Henry VIII* the Globe burned down after sparks from a cannon set the thatched roof alight. It was immediately rebuilt, and continued in operation until all theatres were closed by the Puritans in 1642, after which it was demolished in 1644. American actor Sam Wanamaker had a dream to rebuild the Globe as authentically as possible in Bankside and he set up a trust to raise the finance to do so in 1970. As no plans or drawings existed, the exact details of its construction and location were not known, so considerable research was needed before the design by Theo Crosby could be finalised. After a Herculean struggle Wanamaker managed to secure a site and raise the construction costs. Building began in 1987 and was completed in 1997. Sadly Wanamaker died in 1993 with little more than half of the main structure complete. The foundations of the original Globe were discovered in 1989 about 200 yards from the current building. Plays

by Shakespeare and his contemporaries are performed as authentically as possible. Actors wear period underwear beneath their costumes, and all male productions are sometimes staged: Rylance, the theatre's first Artistic Director, played Cleopatra in 1998. Performances are given in the afternoons, and in the evenings with simulated daylight, during the summer months. Audience participation by those standing in the yard is encouraged. In 2006 Dominic Dromgoole took over as Artistic Director.

SHAKESPEARE'S GLOBE

Lower Gallery

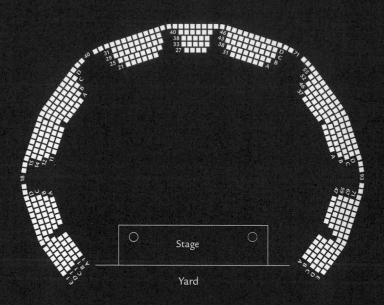

Stage

Yard

50 ▲ *Upper Circle, 28* ▲ *Dress Circle, 4* ▲ *Stalls Circle, 0* ▲ *Yard*
0 ▲ *Foyer,* 👥 *881+600 standing in open Yard*

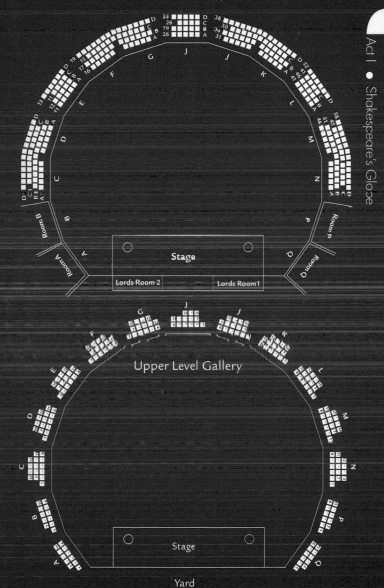

Middle Gallery

Room B

Room A

Room P

Room Q

Stage

Lords Room 2   Lords Room1

Upper Level Gallery

Stage

Yard

Trafalgar Studios

Whitehall SW1Y 2DYR
Box office: 0870 060 6632
Website: www.theambassadors.com
Tube: Charing Cross/Embankment
Train: Charing Cross
Parking: Whitcomb Street/Trafalgar Square
✱ Air Condition
◉ *Splendid Art Deco design details in the auditorium*

Built on the site of Ye Old Ship Tavern, which dated from 1650, it was designed by Edward A Stone, with an interior by French designers Marc-Henri Levy and Gaston Laverdet and opened in 1930 as the Whitehall Theatre. The simple exterior of plain white Portland stone has a temple-like quality that makes a stylistic nod towards the Cenotaph further down Whitehall. In complete contrast the interior is possibly the best example of Art Deco theatre design anywhere, with black walls decorated with silver hatching and floral designs in pastel shades, together with musical instrument and mask motifs in gold, and cubist panels at the sides of the auditorium. Black walls – the first such use in Britain – are decorated with silver hatching and floral designs in pastel shades, together with musical instrument and mask motifs in gold, and cubist panels at the sides of the auditorium. It has been best known for two things – flesh and farce. Phyllis Dixey was the West End's first stripper in non-stop revues *Whitehall Follies* (1942) and *Good Night Ladies* (1944) creating the art of 'ecdysiasm' (as Gypsy Rose Lee called it) talking to the audience as she disrobed. To comply with licensing regulations she had to remain stationary once naked. The flesh era returned after the abolition of censorship, with *Pyjama Tops* (1969), an innocuous comedy into which female nudity was gratuitously (and profitably) injected, and again less successfully in the so-called musical *Voyeurz* (1996). Farce however has been the Whitehall's staple, starting with *Worms Eye View* (1945) with Ronald Shiner and Brian Rix playing a northerner always losing his trousers. Rix went on to produce and often star in *Reluctant Heroes* (1950), *Dry Rot* (1954), *Simple Spyman* (1958), *One For The Pot* (1961), *Chase Me Comrade* (1964) and *Uproar In The House* (1967). It was refurbished and restored reopening in 1985 with J B Priestley's *When We Are Married*. Unusual shows which have played here include John Wells's political comedy *Anyone For Dennis?* (1982) based on the Private Eye magazine column, drag act Hinge And Bracket in *The Importance Of Being Earnest* (1987) and *Rick's Bar Casablanca* (1991), the play on which the film was based. In 2004 it was 'twinned' by extending the circle forward to create one bank of seats facing the existing stage, with a small studio under the circle, and renamed the Trafalgar Studios. Sadly in the process most of the original Art Deco decoration has been covered up.

TRAFALGAR STUDIOS

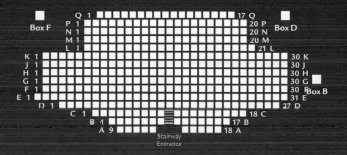

Studio 1

14▲ Rear, 25▼ Front, 🏠 380

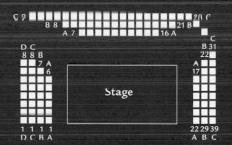

Studio 2

25▼, 1▲ Foyer, 🏠 96

145

Vaudeville

The Strand, WC2R 0NH
Box office: 0870 890 0511
Website: www.nimaxtheatres.com
Tube: Charing Cross/Covent Garden/Leicester Square
Train: Charing Cross
Parking: Bedfordbury/Trafalgar Square
✱ *Air Condition*
◉ *Bust of Shakespeare in a mirrored niche in the Dress Circle foyer*

When the first theatre designed by C J Phipps opened here in 1870, the existing buildings on the Strand were retained and an entrance made through one of them. In 1891 the interior was modified and the present façade of Portland stone, with a first floor loggia and casement windows looking like a private house, was constructed. In 1926 the façade was retained when the interior was gutted and replaced with a design by Robert Atkinson. This eliminated curves, replacing the auditorium's horseshoe shape with a rectangle, but retained some of Phipps' classical ornamentation. Henry Irving made his name here in *The Two Roses* (1870). *Our Boys* (1875) broke all previous London records with a four year run, and was followed by *Our Girls* (1879). Ibsen's *Romersholm* and *Hedda Gabler* both received their first British performances in 1891. The next years saw light comedies featuring actor managers Seymour Hicks and wife Ellaline Terriss, and Charles Hawtrey. For ten years André Charlot presented a series of revues starting with *Samples* (1915), *Buzz-Buzz* (1918) which broke previous revue records through to *Yes* (1923) with Beatrice Lillie. After reconstruction revue returned with *RSVP* and continued for another ten years, including *Charlot's Non-Stop Revue* (1937) after which another refurbishment took place. The comedy *The Chiltern Hundreds* (1947) launched the career of playwright William Douglas Home (returning in 2000) and in 1954 the record breaking musical *Salad Days* (1954) did the same for Julian Slade and Dorothy Reynolds (returning in 1995). It was after a matinée performance of the original production that a young boy called Cameron Mackintosh demanded to go backstage to find out how the magic piano worked. Thus was the course of British musical theatre history transformed. For the Slade/Reynolds team however lightning did not strike again with *Follow That Girl* (1960) or *Wildest Dreams* (1961). Theatre taste had moved on to Arnold Wesker's *Chips With Everything* (1962). Similarly farce, in the shape of *The Man Most Likely To …* (1968) with Leslie Phillips and *Move Over Mrs Markham* (1971), gave way to Alan Ayckbourn's *Absurd Person Singular* (1973), *Woman In Mind* (1987), *Henceforward* (1989) and *Time Of My Life* (1993), Willy Russell's *Shirley Valentine* (1988), and Terry Johnson's *Dead Funny* (1994). *Stomp* (2002) has now become its longest runner.

VAUDEVILLE

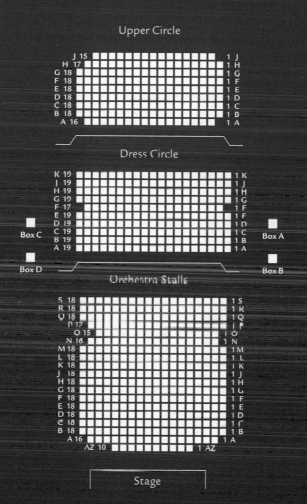

Upper Circle

Dress Circle

Box C · Box D · Box A · Box B

Orchestra Stalls

Stage

59▲ Upper Circle, 27▲ Dress Circle, 5▼ Stalls, 0▲ Foyer, 🎭 690

Victoria Palace

Victoria Street, SW1E 5EA
Box office: 020 834 1317
Website: www.victoriapalacetheatre.co.uk
Tube: Victoria
Train: Victoria
✳ Air Condition   ◁ Infra-red & Induction Loop
♿ Stalls
Parking: Rochester Row/Vauxhall Bridge Road
◉ *The centre of the dome in the auditorium ceiling slides open for increased ventilation*

Built on the site of Moy's Music Hall (later the Royal Standard), which was the first premises in London to hold a music hall license, Victoria Palace was designed by Frank Matcham and opened in 1911. It has a classical white patent stone façade, with a third floor loggia of Ionic columns, surmounted with a Baroque tower crowned with a dome. A mosaic above the entrance depicts two figures, one holding a lyre, the other a mask. A gilded statue of Pavlova on the tower was removed during World War II and disappeared, but was replaced by a replica in 2006. The theatre was built at the height of the music hall boom and owner Alfred Butt wanted it to compete with the best. Although the auditorium is narrower, the interior bears some resemblance to the London Palladium, richly furnished and gilded with Sicilian marble pillars. It opened with variety, and all the best-known names of the period appeared here, joined each Christmas by a fairy play *The Windmill Man* (1921-31). Eventually it moved over to revue with Gracie Fields in *The Show's The Thing* (1929). In 1934 a curiosity called *Young England* became a huge and unlikely hit for the theatre. Written by 84 year old Walter Reynolds as a serious patriotic drama, its melodramatic tale of a scoutmaster unjustly accused of pilfering the scout funds was received as a comedy, with audiences cheering and jeering as the plot unfolded. The management was forced to employ 'chuckers-out' to deal with over excited members of the audience. Other dramas were tried unsuccessfully before its first real hit with Lupino Lane in the musical *Me And My Girl* (1937) which returned in 1944. The Crazy Gang transferred here from the Palladium with *Together Again* (1947), *Knights Of Madness* (1950), *Ring Out The Bells* (1952), *Jokers Wild* (1954), *Crown Jewels* (1959), and their farewell appearance *Young In Heart* (1960). *The Black And White Minstrel Show* (1962), a stage version of the television series, was succeeded by *The Magic Of The Minstrels* (1970), which ran for ten years. It became a musical house with *Annie* (1978), and has since seen *Windy City* (1982), *High Society* (1987), and *Buddy* (1989) plus a number of notorious flops, prior to the hit *Bill Elliott* (2005).

VICTORIA PALACE

Upper Circle

Dress Circle

Stalls

Stage

75 ▲ *Upper Circle, 28* ▲ *Dress Circle, 4* ▼ *Stalls, 0* ▲ *Foyer,* 🎭 *1554*

Wyndham's

Charing Cross Road WC2H oDA
Box office: 0870 950 0925
Website: www.delfont-mackintosh.com
Tube: Leicester Square
Train: Charing Cross
Parking: Lisle Street/Upper St Martin's Lane

✳ Air Condition   ◁ Infra-red

⊙ The house tabs are a fine example of the extravagant Victorian style

Actor manager Charles Wyndham purchased the site after his leading lady and wife Mary Moore had managed to find ten friends to stand guarantors of a £1000 loan each. The first theatre designed by W G R Sprague, it was built on one half of the land in Charing Cross Road and opened in 1899. The Noel Coward in St Martin's Lane, also by Sprague followed in 1903. Both have similar French classical façades with arched balconied windows. The interior is in Louis XVI style in cream, pale blue and gold, with the monograms CW and MM much in evidence. The proscenium is a complete four sided picture frame, above which are two angels holding portraits of Sheridan and Goldsmith in front of a gold winged bust, thought to be of Mary Moore. The ceiling is decorated with Boucher inspired paintings of pastoral scenes. The well-made play has been its trademark starting with Wyndham in *Cyrano de Begerac* and *Mrs Dane's Defence* (1900), and J M Barrie's *Little Mary* (1903). *An Englishman's Home* (1909) written anonymously by 'A Patriot' (actually Gerald du Maurier's brother Guy) about an invasion of England caused a stir and prompted an increase in recruitment in the Territorial Army during pre World War I fervour. Gerald du Maurier appeared in *Raffles* (1914), *Dear Brutus* (1917), *The Choice* (1919), *Bulldog Drummond* (1921) and with Tallulah Bankhead making her London debut in *The Dancers* (1923). Edgar Wallace had an apartment here while his crime dramas were presented which included *The Ringer* (1926) and *Smokey Cell* (1930). In the latter the audience were asked to believe they were to watch an execution by electric chair and were given reproduction journalists cards instead of tickets. Transfers provided many successes including the Players' unexpected hit musical *The Boy Friend* (1954), Theatre Workshop's *A Taste Of Honey* and *The Hostage* (1959) and from the National Theatre, Harold Pinter's *No Man's Land* (1975). Contemporary plays that made a mark were Peter Nichols *Passion Play* (1984), Caryl Churchill's *Serious Money* (1987), David Hare's *Skylight* (1996) and Alan Bennett's The History Boys (2006).

WYNDHAM'S

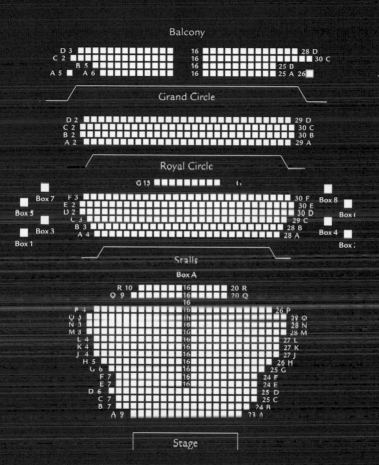

Balcony

Grand Circle

Royal Circle

Stalls

Box A

Stage

43 ▲ Balcony, 21 ▲ Upper Circle, 12 ▲ Dress Circle,
18 ▼ Stalls, 1 ▲ Foyer, ♿ 759

151

Other Venues-
Theatres Off The West End

Almeida
Almeida Street, Islington, N1 1TA
Tel: 020 7359 4404
www.almeida.co.uk

Arts
Great Newport Street, WC1E 7HF
Tel: 020 7836 3334

Greenwich
Crooms Hill, Greenwich, SE10 8ES
Tel: 020 8858 7755
www.greenwichtheatre.org.uk

Hackney Empire
291 Mare Street, Hackney, E8 1EJ
Tel: 020 8985 2424
www.hackneyempire.co.uk

Hammersmith Apollo
Queen Caroline Street,
Hammersmith, W6 9QH
Tel: 0870 606 3400
www.livenation.co.uk

Hampstead
Swiss Cottage Centre, NW3 3EX
Tel: 020 7722 9301
www.hampsteadtheatre.com

Lyric Hammersmith
King Street,
Hammersmith, W6 0QL
Tel: 0870 050 0511
www.lyric.co.uk

New Wimbledon
The Broadway, Wimbledon,
SW19 1QG
Tel: 020 8540 0362
www.theambassadors.com

Richmond
The Green, Richmond, TW9 1QJ
Tel: 0870 060 6651
www.theambassadors.com

The Roundhouse
Chalk Farm Road, NW1 8 EH
Tel: 0870 389 1846
www.roundhouse.org.uk

Soho
21 Dean Street, W1V 6NE
Tel: 870 429 6883
www.sohotheatre.com

Theatre Royal Stratford East
Theatre Square, Stratford, E15 1BN
Tel: 020 8534 0310
www.stratfordeast.com

Tricycle
269 Kilburn High Road, NW6 7JR
Tel: 020 7328 1000
www.tricycle.co.uk

Young Vic
66 The Cut, SE1 8LZ
Tel: 020 7922 2922
www.youngvic.org

Fringe Theatres

Arcola
27 Arcola Street, E8 2DJ
Tel: 020 7503 1646
www.arcolatheatre.com

BAC
Old Town Hall, Lavender Hill,
Battersea, SW11 5TF
Tel: 020 7223 2223
www.bac.org.uk

Barons Court Theatre
28a Comeragh Road, W14 9RH
Tel: 020 8932 4747

Brockley Jack Theatre
410 Brockley Road, SE4 2DH
Tel: 020 8291 6354
www.brockleyjack.co.uk

Bush
58-60 Hampstead Road, NW1 2PY
Tel: 020 7610 4224
www.bushtheatre.co.uk

Camden People's Theatre
100-110 Euston Road, NW1 2AJ
Tel: 0870 060 0100
www.cptheatre.co.uk

Canal Café Theatre
Delamere Terrace, W2 6ND
Tel: 020 7289 6056
www.canalcafetheatre.com

The Chelsea Theatre
World's End Place, King's Road
London, SW10 0DR
Tel: 020 7352 1967
www.chelseatheatre.org.uk

Cochrane
Southampton Row, WC1B 4AP
Tel: 020 7269 1606
www.cochranetheatre.co.uk

The Drill Hall
16 Chenies Street, WC1E 7EX
Tel: 020 7307 5060
www.drillhall.co.uk

Finborough
118 Finborough Road, SW10 9ED
Tel: 0870 400 0838
www.finboroughtheatre.co.uk

Gate Theatre
12 Pembridge Road, W11 3HQ
Tel: 020 7229 0706
www.gatetheatre.co.uk

Hen & Chickens Theatre
109 St Paul's Road, N1 2NA
Tel: 020 7704 2001
www.henandchickens.com

Jermyn Street
16B Jermyn Street, SW1Y 6ST
Tel: 020 7287 2875
www.jermynstreettheatre.co.uk

King's Head
115 Upper Street, Islington, N1 1QN
Tel: 020 7226 1916
www.kingsheadtheatre.org

Landor
70 Landor Road, SW9 9PH
Tel: 020 7737 7276
www.landortheatre.co.uk

Menier Chocolate Factory
51-53 Southwark Street, SE1 1RU
Tel: 020 7907 7060
www.menierchocolatefactory.com

155

New End
27 New End, Hampstead, NW3 1JD
Tel: 0870 033 2733
www.newendtheatre.co.uk

New Players Theatre
The Arches (Off Villiers Street),
WC2N 6NG
Tel: 020 7930 6601
www.newplayerstheatre.com

Old Red Lion
418 St John Street, EC1V 4NJ
www.oldredliontheatre.co.uk

Orange Tree
1 Clarence Street, TW9 2SA
Tel: 020 8940 3633
www.orangetreetheatre.co.uk

Pentameters Theatre
28 Heath Street, NW3 6TE
Tel: 020 7435 3648

Pleasance London
Carpenters Mews, North Road,
Lower Holloway, N7 9EF
Tel: 020 7609 1800
www.pleasance.co.uk

Riverside Studios
Crisp Road, Hammersmith, W6 9RL
Tel: 020 8237 1111
www.riversidestudios.co.uk

Shaw Theatre
100-110 Euston Road, NW1 2AJ
Tel: 0870 033 2600
www.theshawtheatre.com

Southwark Playhouse
Corner of Tooley Street and Bermondsey Street, SE1 2TF
Tel: 0870 0601 761
www.southwarkplayhouse.co.uk

Theatre 503
Latchmere Pub, 503 Battersea Park Road, SW11 3BW
Tel: 020 7978 7040
www.theatre503.com

UCL Bloomsbury
15 Gordon Street, WC1H 0AH
Tel: 020 7388 8822
www.thebloomsbury.com

Union Theatre
204 Union Street, SE1 0LX
Tel: 020 7261 9876
www.uniontheatre.org

White Bear
138 Kennington Park Road, SE11 4DJ
Tel: 020 7793 9193
www.whitebeartheatre.co.uk

Wilton's Music Hall
Graces Alley (Off Ensign Street),
E1 8JB
Tel: 020 7702 2789
www.wiltons.org.uk

Specialist Theatres & Companies

Little Angel
14 Dagmar Passage, Cross Street,
Islington, N1 2DN
Tel: 020 7226 1787
www.theplayerstheatre.co.uk
Home of British puppetry

Newsrevue
Canal Café Theatre, The Bridge
House, Delamere Terrace, W2 6ND
Tel: 020 7289 6054
www.newsrevue.com
The world's longest running topical
comedy show

Polka
240 The Broadway, SW19 1SB
Tel: 020 8543 4888
www.polkatheatre.com
Children's plays and musicals

The Place
17 Duke's Road, WC1H 9AB
Tel: 020 7121 1100
www.theplace.org.uk
Contemporary dance

Unicorn Theatre
147 Tooley Street, SE1 2HZ
Tel: 0870 053 4534
www.unicorntheatre.com
Children's plays and musicals

Concert Halls

Barbican Hall
Silk Street, EC2Y 8DS
Tel: 020 7638 8891
www.barbican.org.uk

Cadogan Hall
5 Sloane Terrace, SW1 9DQ
Tel: 020 7730 4500
www.cadoganhall.com

LSO St Luke's
161 Old Street, EC1V 9NG
Tel: 020 7638 8891
www.lso.co.uk/lsostlukes

Royal Albert Hall
Kensington Gore, SW7 2AP
Tel: 020 7589 8212
www.royalalberthall.com

St John's Smith Square
Smith Square, SW1P 3HA
Tel: 020 7222 1061
www.sjss.org.uk

South Bank Centre (Royal Festival Hall, Queen Elizabeth Hall, Purcell Room)
South Bank, SE1 8XX
Tel: 020 7960 4242
www.sbc.org.uk

Wigmore Hall
36 Wigmore Street, W1H 0BP
Tel: 020 7935 2141
www.wigmore-hall.org.uk

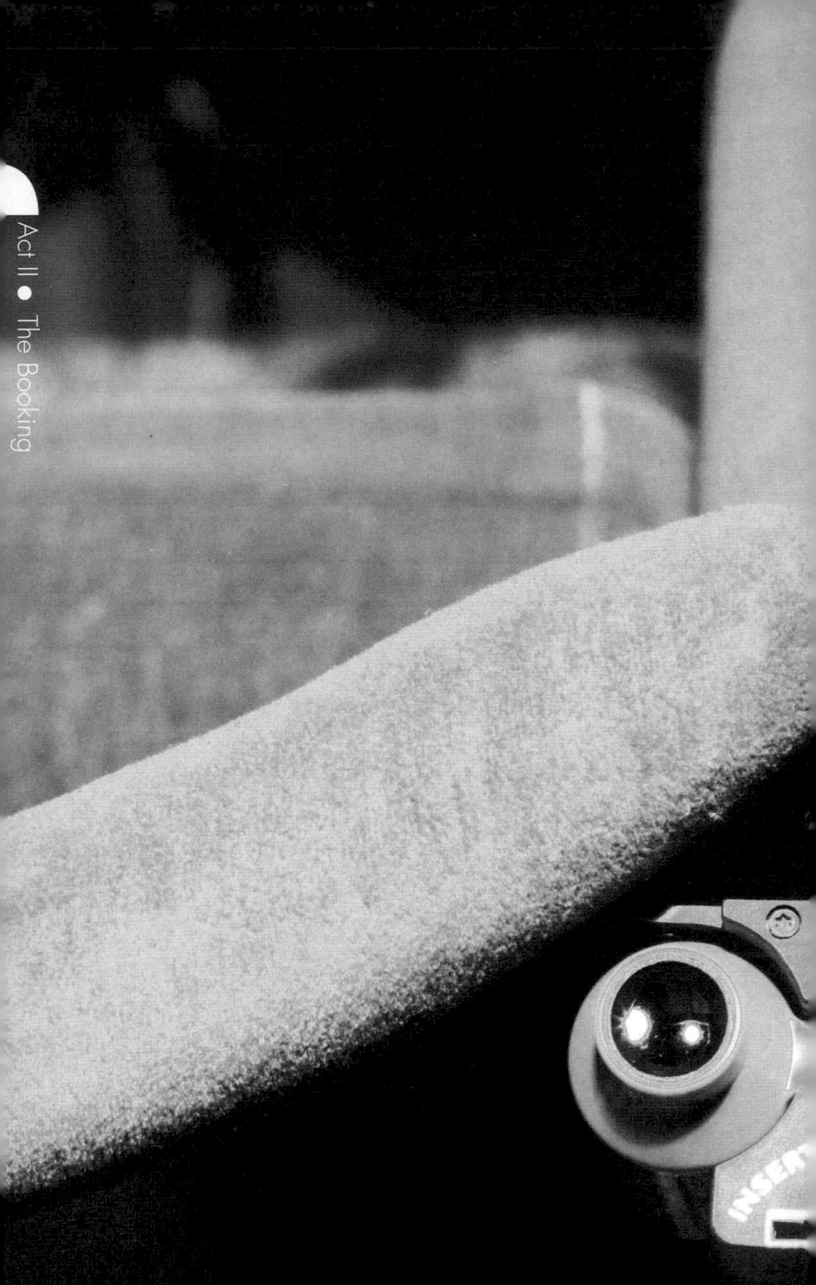

ACT II - THE BOOKING

How To Book

Box Office

◆ Your first port of call should always be the theatre Box Office, either in person, by phone, fax or online. It will have the widest selection of tickets available at the cheapest price. Any ticket booked through a third party will have a service charge of some sort added to the ticket price.

◆ It has never been easier to buy tickets than it is today. Most theatre Box Offices now offer a 24hr/7day telephone credit card service, so you can call from anywhere in the world at a cheap rate. You can charge tickets to your card, and if there is time they will be posted to you, if not you can collect them at the theatre on the night. Do arrive in plenty of time as there may be a queue, and you will need to bring the credit card with you and sign a receipt. Some theatres may charge a service fee for using a card but will advise you of this at the time of the booking.

◆ Most theatres and ticket agents now also offer online ticketing. You can search their availability live, enter your credit card details, and on completion of the transaction, you will generally be given a reference number. Tickets will be posted out or held for collection. Always take the seat numbers and reference number with you when you collect from the Box Office. Some theatres operate what is technically an email postal booking. You will be asked to fill in a form with your requirements and credit card details, and email it to the theatre. They will fulfil your request and email you confirmation. Again tickets will be posted out or held for collection.

◆ You can also reserve tickets by phone (usually for 3 days) and send payment by cheque, postal order or theatre tokens, enclosing a stamped addressed envelope, or pay in person at the theatre. Tickets will not normally be held until the day of performance unless paid for.

◆ Box Offices are generally open to personal callers from 10.00am until 8.00pm or the start of the evening performance. You can usually pay by Sterling cash, credit card, debit card, Sterling cheque (supported by a guarantee card), Sterling travellers cheques or theatre tokens.

There was originally no advance booking or numbered seats and each part of the theatre had a separate entrance. Audiences simply paid on arrival and sat where they liked within the level. The first tickets with numbers on were introduced in 1884. In Victorian times producers believed in large crowds at low prices, hence theatres were bigger and audiences crammed in. They also offered a wider price range, as the difference between the cheapest and the most expensive seats was much greater than today. To sit in the Gallery then cost one sixth of the price of a seat in the Dress Circle, whereas today it is more like one third.

◆ Theatre tokens, which are exchangeable at all London theatres, can be purchased at Box Offices, main bookshop chains, or by credit card from the Society Of London Theatre web site or the 24hr Tokenline.

◆ Unless there is a performance Box Offices are closed on Sundays. On Bank Holidays these times may vary and there may even be no performance. If booking for future performances, it is always best to avoid the half hour immediately before a performance starts, both at matinees and evenings. The windows will be very busy with people collecting tickets, and so you may have to wait. Box Office staff will offer you the best seats available at the time of your booking.

◆ Performances are generally Mondays to Saturdays, with matinées midweek on a Tuesday, Wednesday or Thursday, and on Saturday. Sunday performances have not really taken off in London, and there are rarely more than one or two shows that have substituted a Sunday matinée for Monday night. Evening performances generally start between 7.30pm and 8.00pm. Before World War II shows started later as in European countries – hence Noel Coward's one act play programmes *Tonight At 8.30*. The three auditoria of the National Theatre stagger their starting times at 7.15pm, 7.30pm and 7.45pm to spread the crush. Matinées generally commence between 2.30pm and 3.00pm, although occasionally Saturday matinées may start between 4.00pm and 5.00pm. With skilful planning and a pair of trainers you can sometimes fit in three shows in one day.

House Seats & Returns

◆ Contrary to popular opinion, apart from *Dirty Dancing* or *Billy Elliot,* there are seats available for most West End shows on Mondays to Thursdays from the Box Office on the day of performance. Of course if you want front row centre Dress Circle on Saturday night you will need to book ahead – some months in the case of the big musicals.

> ***Star Tip:*** Good seats usually go on sale on the day of the performance, as the Producer's House Seats are released and unsold ticket agents allocations are marked back. This usually happens either as the Box Office opens at 10.00am or at around 11.00am. Sometimes these seats are available by phone, but on Saturdays and for shows that are almost sold out these may be restricted to sales at the Box Office window. It is always worth trying at the theatre in person if you can. The Royal National Theatre and the Royal Shakespeare Company hold some tickets back for sale on the day at the theatre only.

◆ There is a faxback service providing seating availability information for the current day's performance. Just dial 09069 111 311 from the handset or keypad of your fax machine. This is a premium rate service, costing £1 per minute, and lasting approximately two minutes.

◆ At sold out performances there is usually a queue for returns. These are tickets which people have bought previously but are unable to use, and ask the Box Office to resell on their behalf. For the big shows seats are often purchased months in advance.

> *There is an apocryphal story of the first ever empty seat at a matinee of the original production of My Fair Lady, when it had been standing room only for months. The manager asks the lady next to it if she knows why it is unoccupied. Woman: "I booked the tickets nine months ago for my husband and I, but unfortunately he has since died." Manager: "Couldn't anyone else from you family have come with you?" Woman: "Oh no - they're all at the funeral."*

◆ The queue for returns usually starts about 1-2 hours before the performance. Tickets must be paid for in cash and may be restricted to one per person. Check with the Box Office for their policy.

Disabilities

◆ If you have a disability, most theatres have a specialist to help with your needs when making a booking. Given that the majority of London theatres are listed Victorian or Edwardian buildings conditions are not ideal but they do the best they can. Some street level access is usually available, and seats can be removed to accommodate wheelchairs, but this must be requested when making a booking. Most theatres have either an infra-red or induction loop sound amplification system. Guide dogs are not generally allowed into the auditorium, but are willingly looked after by the front of house staff. Usually a reduced price is offered for yourself and an escort or carer, and an attendant will be assigned to assist.

◆ Signed, audio described and subtitled performances are given regularly. Signed Performances In Theatre provides information on signed performances. Vocaleyes provides a programme of live audio described performances. Stagetext provides a programme of open-captioned performances.

◆ The Shape Ticket Scheme gives disabled and elderly people access to reduced price tickets, as well as providing transport and escorts to theatre and music events. There is a £25.00 annual membership fee, which includes a monthly newsletter.

◆ Artsline provides an information and advice service for disabled people on London's arts and entertainment, as does the National Disability Arts Forum. Radar provides advice and information on general access.

◆ A booklet detailing facilities, Access Guide To London's West End Theatres is published by the Society Of London Theatre and is available free at Box Offices or by post from SOLT. This information is also available on SOLT's web site, together with a listing of forthcoming signed, audio described and subtitled performances.

Parking

On-street parking meters and single yellow line restrictions apply between
8.30am and 6.30pm Monday to Saturday throughout most of the West End
(City of Westminster and Borough of Camden). Generally, after 6.30pm
and at any time on Sunday, you may park free of charge on meters and on
single yellow lines, but always check to be sure.

The Society Of London Theatre and Westminster City Council run a
scheme offering a 50% discount on the standard casual rate tarrif for an
unlimited period at MasterPark car parks seven days a week. Simply get your
car park ticket stamped at the theatre and present it with your ticket stub
when paying. Car parks operating this scheme are situated in the vicinity
of Cambridge Circus, Cavendish Square, Poland Street, Rochester Row,
Trafalgar Square and Whitcomb Street. Valid only to customers arriving
after 9am and leaving before midnight for the date of the performance. For
further information or a free car park map call 0800 243348.

A Theatreland Coach Parking scheme offers designated set down and pick
up bays. A leaflet with a map showing the bays is available at theatres and
from the Transport for London web site.

Ticket Agents

Most major ticket agencies also offer a 24hr/7day telephone credit card
service and/or online booking. The larger agencies have an allocation of
seats at each performance, so that if the Box Office is sold out, they may
be able to help you. If you book with an agent, they should tell you the
face value of the ticket, the location of the seat, and if the view of the
stage is restricted in any way. They will generally charge a service fee, but
reputable agents will advise you of this at the time of booking, and it will
not exceed 25%.

An alliance of reputable agents called STAR - Society of Ticket Agents and
Retailers - works on a similar basis to the ABTA travel agents association.
It has a code of conduct to which all its members must abide. You are
strongly advised not to deal with anyone who is not a member.

Touts

Beware of ticket touts or scalpers. If you are not told the face value of the ticket, the location of the seat, and if the view of the stage is restricted in any way do not buy. Never buy from someone in the street, and beware of the proliferation of small outlets in the vicinity of the Leicester Square Official Half Price Ticket Booth (the clock tower pavilion centrally located in the south of the Square).

If you purchase the ticket in person, always make sure you have seen the ticket and the location on a seating plan before paying. It is not illegal to charge a service fee, but it is illegal to remove or change the face value on a ticket. Never pay for a ticket in person and arrange to collect it later from the theatre, unless you receive a printed agency voucher, with full company details, and the seat number and price on it. Tickets purchased from an unauthorised dealer may be forged or stolen, in which case in addition to being overcharged, you will not be allowed into the theatre. If you feel that you have been misled by an agent please let the Society Of London Theatre know.

I was once working in the Box Office of The Phantom Of The Opera when a Spanish couple came to the window with a sheet torn from a duplicate book on which was written "Seat two people" for which they had paid £200 to someone in the street. As the performance was sold out, including all the returns by the time of their arrival, sadly there was nothing we could do but turn them away.

Nowadays touts are no longer restricted to guys in shabby anoraks haranguing the line at the Half Price Ticket Booth. They now operate web sites as well, so always check that the face value and service charge is clearly stated, and make sure any site you visit has the STAR logo on it.

Royal Opera House

Where To Sit

The part of the theatre where the audience sits is the auditorium. Most London auditoria have three levels. Some have four and the Peacock and Prince of Wales have only two. The higher the level, the steeper the slope (or rake) of the seats to improve sightlines.

Stalls

The lowest part, nearest the stage is the Stalls. Americans call it the Orchestra. The Stalls is the largest area of the auditorium. If you like to be close to the actors so you can see them 'warts and all', then this is for you. The rear half of the Stalls will be under the levels above, the overhang of which may restrict the view of the stage if the set is very tall. As set designers have grown to see their job as producing a "WOW!" from the expensive seats rather than a decent view from the cheap ones, this is inclined to happen more often than it used to.

Dress Circle

The second level is the Dress Circle. Sometimes this is known as the Royal Circle because the Royal Box is on this level. Americans call it the Mezzanine or Balcony. This makes it easier for ticket touts to sell them tickets marked Balcony (which is the fourth level and consequently the worst in the house) for a huge amount, because they think they are buying the best. Many people claim that the Dress Circle is the best place from which to see a show – in a slightly elevated position looking down on the actors.

Until recently there were usually three ticket prices in the Stalls, depending on how close to the stage you were, and two in each of the Circles. This has now generally been reduced to one price per level, as on Broadway, with possibly the back row or two of the Stalls, which may be affected by the overhang of the Dress Circle, at a second price. Obviously the back row in the larger theatres cannot be as good a view as the front, so do check exactly where tickets are located when buying. Top price no longer guarantees best view.

Upper Circle

The third level is the Upper Circle. Not to be confused with the upper class. As Dame Edna Everage says: *"I'm going to look at you paupers just once because that's all you get for what you paid"*. These are the cheap seats (inasmuch as any are cheap nowadays) – perhaps cheaper is more accurate. They are furthest away from the stage looking more steeply down. There is not much to be said about this level, as there is often not much to be seen from it.

Most London theatres were built before civil engineering reached the sophistication of cantilevering, thus there are pillars to keep the upper levels up. Hence the music hall comedian's line *"Don't clap too loud it's a very old building"*. The worst example is probably The Old Vic with 17 pillars in three levels. Many theatres have four pillars repeated on each level. All seats deemed to offer a restricted view by the producer are sold as such at a reduced rate. Experience may bring you to the conclusion that the first requirement of being a producer is to be able to see round corners.

Balcony

If there is one, the fourth level really is called the Balcony. Frequently this has a separate entrance from the rest of the theatre. This dates back to when this level was called the Gallery, and seating here was unbookable unnumbered benches, sold on admission, with the soundest of wind and limb racing up the stairs to claim the front row. It would be nice to find that kind of commitment in audiences nowadays. The queue for returns for Dirty Dancing or Billy Elliot, braving the rain and snow for three hours is the only comparable thing. The view from the Balcony of Drury Lane is the top of the actors heads, and mist or low cloud can be a problem. People who suffer from vertigo usually return ashen faced to the Box Office before the show has even begun. To give some sense of scale, the Balcony of Drury Lane contains more seats than the entire auditorium of the Fortune Theatre which faces its stage door.

Star Tip: The view from the centre blocks of the Balcony at Her Majesty's is very good value as it is not too high, since the theatre has only half the capacity of most of the four level theatres.

Boxes

On each level adjoining the stage there are usually Boxes, seating anything from 2 to 6 people. These are called "The Ash Trays" by comedians such as the one referred to earlier. Remember that Boxes were built to be seen in, rather than to see from. In a traditional Victorian horseshoe shaped auditorium they actually face slightly away from the stage. At best they offer a sideways on view, at worst they are restricted. Boxes are generally the same price as other seats, and each seat is sold individually – you only have the box to yourself if you pay for all of them. When you do have the Box exclusively, if the performance is less than riveting you can misbehave in relative privacy. Do try not to disturb the actors though – a couple in a box at the Apollo ended up with more people watching them than the stage. Nowadays Boxes are often used for lighting and sound equipment, and so are not on sale.

When the London Palladium first opened, the quest for novelty saw a Box to Box telephone system installed. If patrons recognised friends in another Box across the auditorium they were able to engage them in conversation without the effort of walking all the way round.

In traditional West End theatres at Dress Circle level and, access permitting, usually on the auditorium right, there is the Royal Box. This frequently has a separate entrance direct from the street so that the Monarch does not have to mix with the hoi polloi. The last word in Royal comfort was installed at the London Coliseum. An entire Royal Box was built on runners so that the Monarch could enter it direct from the street and glide into position in the auditorium. The first time it was called upon, to perform for Edward VII, it failed to work and has never been tried since. Adjoining the Royal Box is the Royal Retiring Room which allows the Monarch and their entourage to refresh themselves in private.

Because of their age, restrictions of site, building regulations at the time of construction and listed building status, London West End theatres may seem quaint by current standards. Nevertheless they are masterpieces of Victorian or Edwardian ingenuity. In many theatres the Stalls is below ground level because of height restrictions when they were built – all the Shaftesbury Avenue theatres for instance. The exception is the New London which was built in the 1970s where the Stalls is at second floor level with the foyer on the first floor approached by escalators. None have lifts except the new Sadler's Wells, the refurbished Royal Opera House, and Prince of Wales as well as theatres that are part of a complex, such as the National and the Barbican. Be aware that climbing to the Balcony of Drury Lane is a feat comparable to reaching the dome of St Paul's cathedral.

Not to be outdone by anyone else, Drury Lane effectively has two Royal Boxes, dating back to when George III and the Prince Of Wales were not on the best of terms. Having had an altercation on the stairs, in order that they didn't meet in future, they had a box each. The box on the left of the theatre is the Royal Box, decorated with the royal coat of arms, and on right the is the Prince Of Wales Box, decorated with the Prince Of Wales feathers. Similarly the staircases leading from the foyer to the Rotunda are still named the King's Side and the Prince's Side. George V knighted actor manager Frank Benson in the Royal Retiring Room at Drury Lane using a prop sword after a matinée of Julius Caesar in 1916.

Discounts And Special Offers

The days are past when producers could simply put the name of the show and its stars up on the marquee outside the theatre, and wait for people to beat a path to their door. Like all other businesses, theatres now have to sell themselves. This can work to the benefit of audiences, as there are now a range of price options producers use which you can take advantage of.

u On Mondays to Thursdays and for matinées there may be Standby reductions available for Students, Senior Citizens and Unemployed (UB40 holders). Generally these are any remaining best seats for about 1/3 of the normal price. These are usually available for cash only, from 1 hour before the performance, one per person and are not bookable. Check with the Box Office for their policy

◆ tkts are the only Official Half Price and Discount Theatre Ticket Booths in London, run by the Society Of London Theatre. tkts offer usually top price tickets at half their face value (plus a service charge of £2.50) for a wide range of shows on the day of performance only. Availability is posted on boards each day. The main tkts booth is in the clock tower pavilion in Leicester Square. Beware of imitators in the side roads around the Square. It opens Mondays to Saturdays at 10.00am for matinee and evening performances, with last sales at 7.00pm, and on Sundays from 12noon to 3.30pm. The second tkts booth is located at the Canary Wharf Docklands Light Railway Station on Platforms 4/5. It is open Mondays to Saturdays from 10.00am to 3.30pm. Payment must be in cash, theatre tokens or by credit or debit card – personal and travellers cheques are not accepted.

◆ ShowPairs circulate special offers to businesses, posting out vouchers usually offering two seats for the price of one. Various conditions apply which are printed on the vouchers. Tickets are only bookable direct with the Box Office, usually for Monday to Thursday performances and for a specific period of a month. The vouchers must be sent with payment or exchanged when tickets are collected. You can join the scheme for free, but remember offers are always subject to availability.

◆ ShowSavers send out special offers by email and fax, sometimes with very big reductions for shows and concerts. There is also an online listing of these offers on the ShowSavers web site, and a weekly email Newsletter with a summary of the current deals. Again tickets must be booked direct with the Box Office or a ticket agent, but a copy of the email or fax is not required. You can join the scheme for free on the web site, but remember offers are always subject to availability.

◆ Get Into London Theatre is an annual initiative, designed to encourage new and young theatregoers to experience theatre in London. Discounted tickets are available for over 60 shows, including opera, ballet and dance, in over 40 venues, encompassing West End, fringe and suburban theatres. Prices vary according to the venue for selected performances from January to March. Restaurants also take part with accompanying deals, hotels offer special mini-breaks, and there are extra special offers for 16-25 year olds.

◆ Ambassador Theatre Group's Upstage club entitles members to promotional discounts, a dedicated booking phone line, and free use of Royal Room at their theatres. Annual membership costs £15.

◆ The Royal National Theatre and English National Opera at the London Coliseum offer some cheap tickets to personal callers at the Box Office only from 10.00am on the day of performance. These may be restricted to two per person. At the Royal Court Theatre all seats are £10.00 on Monday nights.

> **Star Tip:** You may also be able to sit in the best seats at a cheaper price by strategic buying. Often at midweek matinées in less busy times of the year, Upper Circle and/or Balcony levels are closed and you will be reseated in the best seats. Alternatively you can buy restricted view seats and move to an empty full view seat as the house lights go down or, if you are faint of heart, at the interval (Of course I didn't tell you that). Be careful to avoid half-term weeks when business shoots up.

◆ Some ticket agents now offer show and meal deals, combining usually (but not always) a top price ticket, with a meal before or after the show at a nearby restaurant, for just the price of the ticket – and sometimes even less.

◆ Group reductions are usually available for Monday to Thursday performances and sometimes for Fridays and Saturdays. The minimum size of groups and prices vary so check with the Box Office but can be from as few as six. Some theatres have established a group booking office and send out regular newsletters with information and offers. Reservations can usually be held for up to four weeks. All ticket agents will handle group bookings, some make it their speciality.

◆ Most shows play a week or so of previews before the press night, although sadly no longer at half-price. There are still some reductions, and they offer the extra excitement – and danger – of the show being played in. Adding the audience is the final element in creating a show, and until it happens no one knows quite how things will turn out. It is always interesting to make your own mind up before the critics see it.

Star Tip: If you want to be part of the first night, it is often possible to buy tickets a day or two beforehand, once the producer has allocated his requirements. There may be returns just before the show starts, and if the Box Office staff are feeling particularly kind-hearted they may even give away unused complimentary tickets. Remember that first nights usually begin at 7.00pm.

◆ Some producing and receiving theatres such as the Barbican, English National Opera, National, Royal Court, Royal Opera House, Sadler's Wells, Almeida and Donmar Warehouse run mailing lists. Those on the list receive regular news letters and occasional special offers, although some theatres have a joining fee.

◆ If your interests embrace the arts generally, then The London Pass offers free entry to a number of cultural institutions and visitor attractions, saving both time and money. Available for 1, 2, 3 and 6 days, it can also include public transport.

VIP TICKETS ◆ Royalty often sit in the Dress Circle rather than the Royal Box nowadays. As a result, the Royal Box and the Royal Retiring Room can be hired for VIP parties (although hardly <u>that</u> important if you have to pay for it). So if you are planning an extra special night out, you can book a VIP package which will guarantee you best seats, drinks and/or canapés in the Retiring Room before, during and/or after the show, your own attendant to tend to your needs, and free programmes and brochures. Packages are tailored to individual requirements.

THEATRE BREAKS ◆ You can now find Theatre Break packages that combine accommodation with tickets for shows and concerts. These can be tailored to individual requirements, with both midweek or weekend availability. Usually hotel prices are keener at the weekends, but tickets are cheaper and more readily available during the week. Again both the theatres themselves and agents who make it their speciality have a variety of packages available. It is worth shopping around.

Theatre Tours

If you have ever wondered how a theatre works, a number of London theatres now offer backstage tours: Barbican, Theatre Royal Drury Lane, Duke of York's, Theatre Royal Haymarket, Her Majesty's, London Coliseum, London Palladium, Prince Edward, Prince of Wales, Royal Court, National Theatre, New London, Royal Opera House, Sadler's Wells, Shakespeare's Globe, and also the Royal Albert Hall and The Roundhouse These generally last about an hour and a quarter. Some run at regular times throughout the day Monday to Saturday - excluding matinee afternoons, while others are only weekly or monthly. Shakespeare's Globe and Theatre Royal Drury Lane tours also run on Sundays. Advance booking is always recommended, as the size of groups is restricted, and sometimes required. Young children are not admitted. These are working theatres and therefore access cannot be guaranteed to all areas of the buildings at all times.

Free Sources Of Information

The Official London Theatre Guide
www.OfficialLondonTheatre.co.uk
Fortnightly guide produced by the Society Of London Theatre available at all West End theatres and information centres or posted to you on subscription.

London Planner
www.visitlondon.com
Monthly guide produced by the British Tourist Authority with comprehensive entertainment listings available from hotels and information centres.

What's On Stage
Monthly magazine with features and listings available at all West End theatres.

Metro
Daily newspaper with entertainment listings distributed at rail and underground stations during the morning rush hour.

thelondonpaper
Daily newspaper with entertainment listings distributed at rail and underground stations during the evening rush hour.

Journals and Magazines

Time Out
Universe House, 251 Tottenham Court Road, W1P 0AB
Tel: 020 7813 3000
www.timeout.com
Weekly listings magazine.

What's On In London
Strand Magazines, Duchy House, 133 Strand, WC2R 1HH
Tel: 08450 132931
www.whatsoninlondon.co.uk
Weekly listings magazine.

The Stage
47 Bermondsey Street, London, SE1 3XT
Tel: 020 7403 1818
www.thestage.co.uk
Weekly newspaper of the British theatre.

Theatre Record
131 Sherringham Avenue, N17 9RU
Tel: 020 8808 3656
www.theatrerecord.com
Fortnightly magazine reproducing all national newspaper reviews of West End and regional shows.

Celebrity Bulletin
Rooms 203-209, 93-97, Regent Street, W1R 7TA
Tel: 020 7439 9840
www.celebrityservice.com
Daily listing of celebrity movements world wide, including the stars who are in London and what they are doing.

Dance & Dancers
83 Clerkenwell Road, EC1R 5AR
Tel/Fax: 020 7813 1049
Monthly magazine with reviews and features about British dance.

Dance Now
The Old Bakery, 4 Lenten Street, Alton, Hampshire, GU34 1HG
Tel: 01420 86138
www.dancebooks.co.uk
Quarterly magazine with reviews and features about all kinds of dance.

Dancing Times
Clerkenwell House, 45-47 Clerkenwell Green, EC1R oEB
Tel: 020 7250 3006
www.dancing-times.co.uk
Monthly magazine with reviews and features about British dance.

Musical Stages
PO Box 8365, London, W14 oGL
Tel/Fax: 020 7603 2221
www.musicalstages.co.uk
Quarterly magazine with reviews and features about British musical theatre.

Opera Magazine
36 Black Lion Lane, W6 9BE
Tel: 020 8563 8893
www.opera.co.uk
Monthly magazine with reviews and features about British opera.

Opera Now
Rhinegold Publishing, 241 Shaftesbury Avenue, WC2E 8TF
Tel: 020 7333 1720
Bi-monthly magazine with reviews and features about British opera.

Plays International
The performing Arts Trust, 33A Lurline Gardens, SW11 4DD
Tel/Fax: 020 7720 1950
www.playsinternational.org.uk
Bi-monthly magazine with reviews of British and international theatre

Sounds Great!
Sounds Great, Stag's Corner, Hurtmore Road, Godalming, GU7 9RA
Tel: 01483 427 965
www.soundsgreat.co.uk
10 issues a year with listings of classical concerts and events in London and south east England.

Ticket Outlets

Theatre Owners & Operators

Ambassador Theatre Group
Duke Of York's Theatre,
St Martin's Lane, WC2N 4BG
Tel: 020 7854 7000
www.theambassadors.com
Group Sales: 0870 060 6644
Education: 020 8290 8264
Upstage Club: 0870 060 6634

Delfont Mackintosh Theatres
Novello Theatre,
Aldwych, WC2B 4LD
Tel: 020 7379 4431
www.delfontmackintosh.co.uk
Group Sales: 0870 850 9199
Education: 0870 850 9171
VIP: 0870 950 0950

Really Useful Theatres
22 Tower Street, WC2H 9TW
Tel: 020 7240 0880
www.rutheatres.com
Group Sales: 0870 899 3342
Theatre Breaks: 0870 143 2201
VIP: 020 8795 9899

tkts – (Official Half Price Ticket Booths)
Clock Tower Building, Leicester Square, WC2
& Platforms 4/5, Canary Wharf Docklands Light Railway Station, EC14
www.tkts.co.uk

Ticket Agencies

Abbey Box Office
55 Wilton Road, SW1V 1DE
Tel: 020 7798 9200
& 30 Jubilee Market,
Covent Garden, WC2E 8BE
Tel: 020 7836 3337
www.abbeyboxoffice.co.uk

Keith Prowse
Britain & London Visitor Centre,
1 Regent Street, SW1Y 4XT
Tel: 020 7808 3871

Rakes - London Theatre Bookings
90-98 Shaftesbury Avenue, W1D 5EB (Office Only)
& 4 Irving Street, WC2
& 31 Coventry Street, W1V 7FH
& Unit 1, The Hippodrome, Cranbourn Street, WC2 7JN
& 23 St Martins Court, WC2A 6GH
& 188 Shaftesbury Ave, WC2H 8JN
Tel: 020 7851 0300
www.londontheatrebookings.com

Stargreen Concert Box Office
20 Argyle Street, W1F 7TT
Tel: 020 7734 8932
www.stargreen.com

West End Theatre Bookings - UK Tickets
The APE House, Parklands, Guildford, GU2 9JX (Office Only)
& Leicester Square Tube Station, WC2
& 35 Long Acre, WC2
Tel: 0870 042 1004
www.uktickets.co.uk

Phone/Online

Keith Prowse
62 Long Acre, WC2E 9JQ
(Office Only)
Tel: 0870 840 1111
www.keithprowse.com

See Tickets
Manor House, 21 Soho Square,
W1D 3QP (Office Only)
Tel: 0870 264 3333
www.seetickets.com

Ticketmaster
16 Leicester Square, WC2H 7LR
(Office Only)
Tel: 0870 590 0123
www.ticketmaster.co.uk

Albemarle
5th Floor, Medius House, 63-69
New Oxford Street, WC1A 1DG
(Office Only)
Tel: 0870 240 2978
www.albemarle-london.com

Fenchurch
90-98 Shaftesbury Avenue, W1D 5EB
Tel: 020 7851 0300
www.theatreticket.co.uk

Lashmars
1st Floor New Burlington Street,
W1S 2JD (Office Only)
Tel: 020 7494 1767
www.londontheatre.co.uk/lashmars

Groups

Groupline
22-24 Torrington Place, WC1E 7HF
Tel: 020 7580 6793
www.groupline.com

Theatre Breaks

Bill Wright's Capital Breaks
The Pines, Woodhead Road
Holmfirth, HD9 2SA
Tel: 01484 682255
www.londonbreaks.com

Latest Events
279-283 Greenwich High Road, 3rd
Floor, London, SE10 8NL
Tel: 0208 269 4832
www.latestevents.com

Superbreak
60 Piccadilly, York, YO1 9WX
Tel: 0871 700 4381
www.superbreak.com

Theatre Breaks
PO Box 1, St Albans, AL1 4ED
Tel: 01727 840244
www.theatrebreaks.com

Sarastro

ACT III - THE NIGHT

Where To Go And What To Do

A walk through the theatre; etiquette, conventions and terms explained

◆ If you are spending a fortune on tickets – and nowadays most producers don't give you any other option – you want to make sure you get the most out of your evening. Be certain to allow yourself plenty of time to reach the theatre, especially if you have not been there before. London theatres are spread over a much wider area than Broadway, and it's easy to take a wrong turn if you are not familiar with the territory.

◆ Bear in mind that you will never find a parking space near the theatre, that traffic can clog up the streets delaying buses or taxis, and that the natural state for a tube train is stationary in a tunnel. On the subject of taxis, don't forget the (surely) apocryphal story of the taxi driver delivering someone late at *The Mousetrap*, whose passengers fled without giving him a tip, so he responded with a tip of his own, shouting after them "The ********* did it!".

◆ Much better to arrive early and have time to admire the fabulous architecture – sometimes it's the best part of the evening! If you miss the start of the show you may have to wait for a suitable break before you can be seated.

◆ There is no longer any dress code for audiences at London theatres, and Black Tie is unusual, even for first nights. The only recommendation therefore is that whatever you wear should not provoke a response from the attendants along the lines of: *"What have you come as?"*. Unless of course you are attending The Rocky Horror Show, where fancy dress is not only permitted, but considered by some to be obligatory.

◆ You enter via the Foyer where you used to be welcomed by a Commissionaire or link man. I knew of one whose opening gambit was "Enter a different world". Sadly this is no longer the case, but you may get a weak smile from the manager (if it's the regular one's night off). In the Foyer you will find the Box Office – except for the London Palladium where the Box Office has a separate entrance to the left of the main doors. This dates from the time when the Palladium presented twice nightly variety with no advance booking so they had to process large crowds of people very quickly. Usually the Box Office has different windows for buying tickets and collecting prepaid ones. Sometimes the prepaid desk is on the opposite side of the Foyer to help with crowd control.

◆ If you are collecting tickets aim to arrive in plenty of time. Five hundred people all trying to collect their tickets in the last five minutes before Curtain Up can cause delays. It also offers no opportunity for the Box Office staff to sort out any difficulties if you have booked through an agent and there is a problem. Incidentally, the start of the show is always called Curtain Up regardless of whether or not there is a curtain, and if there is one, in which direction it moves – nowadays curtains can go down as well as up. Once you have your ticket you can confirm which part of the theatre you are in. You may need to go back outside to a separate entrance if you are in the Balcony or Upper Circle. A few last vestiges of the British class system still remain.

◆You can then explore the building. Drury Lane has many paintings and sculptures dotted around the Front Of House – the term for the public part of the theatre. In the Royal Opera House the Grand Staircase and the Crush Bar boast huge allegorical paintings. The corridor at the rear of the Dress Circle of the Olivier Theatre at the National has a permanent exhibition about its history from 1848, which includes plans and designs for the various theatres proposed to house the company but were never built.

◆ There are Bars on all levels - sometimes two. There are toilets on all levels - again sometimes **only** two. Because most theatres are listed Victorian buildings, toilets are not so plentiful as in modern ones. The Bars are generally open from 45 minutes before the performance starts, and some offer sandwiches, cakes and coffee as well as drinks. Only the Barbican, the National, the Royal Opera House and Shakespeare's Globe have restaurants. Bars range from the Stalls at the Ambassadors which enjoys the intimacy of a tube train in the rush hour, to the sumptuous Grand Saloon at Dress Circle level at Drury Lane, the grandest theatre Bar in the world. It's almost worth the price of admission to enter there alone.

Star Tip: The Stalls Bar at the Palace Theatre has an adjoining picture gallery with a fascinating collection of photographs and drawings of past productions. At the Adelphi the Front Stalls Bar has a collection of material relating to the works of composer Vivian Ellis and the Side Stalls Bar that of performer Jessie Matthews. At the Prince of Wales the Stalls Bar has a large collection of programmes and stage and costume designs from previous productions. At the Phoenix the Dress Circle Bar contains a collection of Noel Coward memorabilia.

◆ Do order your drinks for the interval in advance. It seems to be a great British tradition not to do this. I don't know why this is – guilt at having too good a time perhaps? Or the suspicion that the Bar staff will walk off into the sunset to start a new life on the proceeds of your drinks order? Theatre Bar prices are high, but not that high! Whatever the reason, most London theatregoers seem to prefer the 'no pleasure without pain' route. They wait until the interval and then jostle each other out of the way, fighting for the attention of the Bar staff, so that (all the ice having gone) they finally raise a glass of tepid liquid to their lips, just as the first bar bell rings to herald the start of Act II. Then they have to knock it back in one gulp. Take my advice – don't join in. Order in advance and avoid the scrum.

Star Tip: Some bars no longer sell wine by the glass but in ¼ bottles (2 glasses) so for the interval, 1 bottle with 2 glasses is perfect.

◆ As you pass into the Auditorium (that's the bit where the seats are) remember that unlike in Broadway theatres, London programmes must be paid for. The first London playbills - literally a simple list of cast and scenes - were issued free to audiences at the Olympia Theatre in 1850. The National and Royal Court still give away free cast lists today. The first programmes as we know them now were introduced at the St James's Theatre in 1869.

◆ In the last few years the quality of material in programmes has improved considerably, and they are better value for money. Programmes are only available in English, but can usually be bought in advance from the Box Office if this is not your first language and you need to do some research before the night - or don't own a torch.

Give a second glance to the person selling you the programme or showing you to your seat, as many are aspiring or resting performers. On a number of occasions people have moved directly from the Auditorium to the Stage of the same theatre - but this will hopefully not happen on the night you are there. The most successful example of this was Nell Gwynne. Originally one of Mrs Mary Meggs's orange sellers in the stalls of Drury Lane, she graduated to the stage in John Dryden's The Indian Emperor in 1665, at the age of 15. King Charles II saw her, fell in love with her, and took her as his mistress.

My favourite story regarding programme copy comes from the days before computerised copysetting was introduced. Then, when metal type was literally set letter by letter, if a printer found an error, the word or phrase was taken out, remade and put back. On one occasion two phrases were switched around when they were put back, with the result that in the description of the show, instead of reading "in a brutal military regime, a bogus Catholic priest is locked overnight in the condemned cell with a Muslim, an atheist and a Jew" actually became "in a brutal military regime, a bogus Catholic priest is locked overnight in the condemned cell with the original London cast of Lock Up Your Daughters" .

◆ To help you find your seat, the numbering in most London theatres starts from low numbers on the Auditorium Right – that is as you face the stage – running to the high numbers on the Auditorium Left.

◆ Usually you will find a small pair of binoculars attached to the rear of the seat in front of you, which with typical delusions of grandeur are known as Opera Glasses. These can be liberated from their clamp by the insertion of an ever increasing number of coins. They usually have a warning on them that they are useless outside the theatre to deter thieves. Unfortunately there is no warning that they are pretty useless inside the theatre too.

◆ As you settle into your seat, remember that for copyright reasons you are not allowed to take photographs, or make video or audio recordings during the performance. If you attempt to do so the attendants will ask you to stop, and the manager may ask you to surrender your equipment for the remainder of the show, which will be returned minus the film or tape.

◆ Also, if you have one with you, turn off your mobile phone or pager. The climax of a recent first night was ruined by one beeping at the crucial moment. The actor Richard Griffiths has stopped performances and admonished perpetrators for their disrespect during various productions. I think we have almost reached the point when mobile devices should be checked at the door – like guns in Western saloons. I recently heard an announcement asking people to turn off a huge list of electrical equipment including egg timers and hair curlers, but said that pacemakers were OK.

Talking of announcements, your heart need not necessarily sink if you hear the words "owing to the indisposition of . . ." During the run of Bennett's play The Lady In The Van two actors 'portrayed' Bennet. When one of them was suddenly absent due to the imminent birth of his child, the audience heard the announcement "at this performance the role of Alan Bennett will be played by Alan Bennett".

◆ After mobile phones, the next most annoying thing about your fellow audience members is likely to be coughing. The critic James Agate wrote in the 1930s that *"only people suffering from acute bronchitis seem to go to West End theatres"*, so it's not a new problem. The old saw was that endless throat clearing was a sign of boredom. Tyrone Guthrie said, after his production of Tamburlaine The Great had spectacularly flopped on its first night, that *"the next morning the notices put the nail in the coughing"*.

◆ One positive development is that sweet paper rustling seems to have almost died out in West End theatres – although they still have warning announcements about it on Broadway. This may be down to the kind of sweets on sale in theatres or perhaps it's a 'healthy eating culture' developing. Either way this is a disappointment for the sound operator I know, who searches through the stalls each night, scavenging for forgotten half full boxes of chocolates and discarded programmes. The chocolates he keeps to sweeten his journey home, and the programmes (provided they are in a suitable condition) he sells for half price to the attendants the next night, for their own entrepreneurial purposes.

◆ Most West End shows are run like efficient military machines with more than competent first and second understudies on standby to cover illness and holidays. This is not always the case. I recall a flu epidemic during the original production of *Jesus Christ Superstar* making it difficult to find 12 apostles for the Last Supper and resorting to females and on one occasion ended up with 13 – I liked to think that these incidents made for interesting theological discussions among the audience in the interval.

◆ There is a mystical line that runs through the theatre. It divides the audience's area Front Of House from the performer's area Backstage. These two worlds meet in one place, the Fourth Wall of their respective areas, defined by the Proscenium Arch – the decorated frame which surrounds the Stage opening. Usually when you take your seat it is filled with the curtain or Tabs, the most extravagant Victorian example of which are to be seen at Wyndhams Theatre.

◆ Musicals usually start with the overture, the magic moment when the house lights dim a little and the theatrical experience takes an anticipatory hold of the audience. Meanwhile backstage panic is sometimes engendered – the equivalent of the realisation that the plane has taken off with the baggage door still open.

◆ An alarming trend on Broadway is for Musical Directors to throw away their sticks (like cripples at an evangelist's meeting) and jig about rather than actually conduct, sometimes for the overture, sometimes for the whole show. Fortunately this has yet to spread to the West End, but if you find yourself at an outbreak do complain to the manager - it's always better to stop an epidemic as early as possible. Incidentally, one advantage of sitting in the front row is that if the show has dull patches you can peruse the MD's reading matter over his or her shoulder. One conductor I know always examines his upcoming entertainment options on the day the Radio Times is published, by working his way through with a highlighter pen.

◆ When the Tabs finally rise, or go 'Out' – i.e. out of the audience's sight – (at the end they fall or come 'In') the performers come on. Once there, if they move away from the audience, they are going 'Upstage', or come towards the audience, 'Downstage'. This is because at one time all stages had a slope or rake to improve sightlines, so the performers had to get used to working on the side of a hill. The only remaining London theatres with a built-in rake are Drury Lane and the Haymarket. Stage Left and Stage Right are the performers left and right as they face the audience – the opposite of Auditorium Left and Auditorium Right.

◆ Owing to the propensity of 19th century theatres to burn down, the Iron or Safety Curtain must be lowered in the interval, to prove that it is in working order. Thus should a fire break out on stage the audience can be sealed off and protected. The performers, being professionals, are permitted by the licensing authority to be fried. At the first night of *The Lady Of Lyons* at the Shaftesbury Theatre in 1888 the Iron, having been lowered could not be raised again, and after an hour the performance was abandoned, as was the entire run. In case you are wondering this was the Shaftesbury theatre which stood in Shaftesbury Avenue almost opposite the Palace (where the Fire Station is now) which was destroyed by World War II bombing. The first Iron was installed in 1800 in Drury Lane (which had previously burnt down in 1672) only to see it destroyed by fire again in 1809. Sometimes Irons are richly painted in keeping with the plasterwork of the surrounding proscenium and boxes, such as the Piccadilly, some feature cherubs as at the Haymarket, others are simply inscribed with the motto, 'For Thine Especial Safety'. The most elaborate are a reproduction of an Italian Renaissance painting at the Phoenix, and a view of the auditorium – complete with audience – at the Victoria Palace.

It used to be possible to order Afternoon Tea to be served in your seat in the interval at matinees. An attendant would arrive with a tray containing a proper earthenware teapot, with loose tea (not teabags), a china cup and saucer, a plate of sandwiches and a slice of Dundee cake - and all for a modest sum. No longer alas. In those days the attendants and bar staff all seemed to be female and past retirement age. I recall seeing one such lady emerge gingerly from the rear Stalls Bar at the Noel Coward with three trays balanced on top of each other and fail to make it with messy consequences.

◆ A further fire prevention precaution is the Drencher. When set off this creates a sheet of water across the width of the Proscenium Arch, again designed to stop fire spreading from the stage into the auditorium, which once started cannot be stopped until the entire contents of the water tank has run through. It can make a very effective finale to a production of *110 In The Shade* – a play and musical about a rainmaker. However, the control for the Iron is always located next to the control for the Drencher and there have been occasions in intervals... Well let's just say it takes an awful lot of mopping up before Act II can start.

◆ If you look up to the ceiling in the Auditorium there is often a central dome. In some theatres such as the Victoria Palace and the Shaftesbury this could be rolled to one side, or opened in half in the interval to increase ventilation on summer nights. This was particularly useful in those building constructed as music halls, where drinking and smoking were de rigeur, but it should be remembered that at one time all theatres allowed smoking in the auditorium.

◆ It is becoming more common nowadays in plays for there to be no interval. Playwrights of today often write pieces of 75 or 90 minutes, and you find yourself back on the pavement by the middle of the evening. This does not indicate that the evening has been a disappointment and the trend is perhaps an acknowledgement that modern audiences are more used to the shorter extent of modern television drama.

◆ The theatre owners don't like shows without an interval – for it is they who receive the entire bar sales, not the show's producers, who are simply 'hiring the hall'. Despite being a full length show, the original Broadway production of the musical Man Of La Mancha was played without an interval so as no to 'break the spell'. When it came here, the management of the Piccadilly Theatre insisted an interval was introduced as part of the hire contract. Indeed, when the producer of another show, which opened to disastrous reviews, wanted to cut their losses and take the show off over-night, the theatre owner said only if the producer paid huge compensation for the bar and programme sales losses during the two week notice period. So the two weeks of performances went ahead.

◆ With a bit of luck (and the consummate skill of the practitioners), you really will be transported to a different world for two and a half hours, and all too soon it will be Curtain Down. Incidentally, I don't know if this is a hangover from the days when the National Anthem was played at the end of cinema and theatre performances – which people tried to avoid by making a dash for the exit – but some audience members start to leave at the end of the last scene, before curtain calls – which is very bad manners. Besides, like the overture, the playout (that's the music the orchestra plays after the curtain calls while the audience is leaving) can sometimes be the best part of the evening.

◆ As you leave theatre you may go past the Stage Door, where at the Pal-ace and Prince Edward you will see the inscription: *"Through this door have passed and will pass some of the greatest stars of the British theatre"*. Hopefully you will think *"Tonight I was privileged to share time with some of them"*. Just remember what a wonderful night you had, tell all your friends, and go to the theatre again soon.

Remember They Can See And Hear You

Nowadays audiences in theatres often behave as though they are at home watching television - although thankfully most don't keep getting up to make a cup of tea. They should perhaps be reminded that unlike television, the actors can see and hear them. Hence the reporting of the following overheard audience comments:

On an actor's entrance: *"Oh no, not him - he's terrible!"*

During David Kernan's heartfelt rendition of a tender ballad in Side By Side By Soldheim: *"Oh look! Turn ups are coming back!"*

About an actress who was knitting while playing Victoria In Victoria And Albert: *"Well she may be the Queen, but the woman can't knit to save her life - she hasn't a clue."*

Following an extended rustle of chocolate wrappers: *"Who's taken the hazelnut fondant?"*

Minicab message on the sound system during The Cherry Orchard: *"Taxi car needed to take a party to the station, is anyone available? (PAUSE) Apparently there's luggage."*

And finally . . . Robert Morley to a fellow actor complaining about an amorous couple in the stalls *"Well, if we can't entertain them, then they have a perfect right to do it for themselves."*

Lyceum Theatre

After The Show (or Before)

Restaurants, Wine Bars & Brasseries, Pubs, Cafés & Tea Venues, Later Entertainment

Eating and drinking establishments come and go at an alarming speed in London, but some institutions continue forever. Here is a selection of my favourites from the long runners popular with theatre people, ranging in price from the smart and expensive to good value budget establishments.

Restaurants

ROYAL BOX (FIRST CLASS)

Café Royal Grill Room
68 Regent Street, W1
020 7439 1855
Gilt mirrors and red velvet "the most beautiful dining room in London" - Cecil Beaton.

The Ivy
1 West Street, WC2
020 7836 4751
www.the-ivy.co.uk
London's 'Sardi's' remains the ultimate theatre rendezvous.

Rules
35 Maiden Lane, WC2
020 7836 5314
www.rules.co.uk
Opened 1798 it claims to be the oldest restaurant in London - game a speciality

The Savoy Grill
The Strand, WC2
020 7592 1600
www.gordonramsay.com
The legendary location has survived the makeover that brought a more contemporary menu.

Simpsons in the Strand
100 The Strand, WC2
020 7836 9112
www.simpsons-in-the-strand.co.uk
Solid traditional British surroundings providing similar food - roasts a speciality.

DRESS CIRCLE (CLUB CLASS)

Joe Allen
13 Exeter Street, WC2
020 7836 0651
www.joeallenrestaurant.com
Even more a part of the theatre scene in London than its New York cousin.

La Barca
80 Lower Marsh, SE1
020 7928 2226
www.labarca.co.uk
Typical traditional Italian service and menu – handy for the National.

Bentley's
11-15 Swallow Street, W1
020 7758 4141
www.bentleys.org
Traditional club style dining room offering outstanding fish dishes.

Bertorelli's
44A Floral Street, WC2
020 7836 3969
www.santeonline.co.uk
Art Deco-with-a-twist decorative style and Italian-basics-with-a-twist food.

Brown's
82-84 St Martin's Lane, WC2
020 7497 5050
www.browns-restaurants.com
A former courthouse with Oxbridge style and Brideshead ambience.

Le Café du Jardin
28 Wellington Street, WC2
020 7836 8769
www.lecafedujardin.com
Modern Mediterranean menu in simple elegant surroundings.

Café Pacifico
5 Langley Street, WC2
020 7379 7728
www.cafepacifico-laperla.com
More Mex than Tex lively cantina atmosphere with modern Mexican menu.

Chez Gerard at the Opera Terrace
45 East Terrace Covent Garden, WC2
020 7379 0666
www.santeonline.co.uk
Inside the conservatory or outside on the terrace on the roof of the old market building.

Christopher's
18 Wellington Street, WC2
020 7240 4222
www.christophersgrill.com
Modern American décor and grill menu - good for steak and fish.

The Criterion
224 Piccadilly, W1
020 7930 0488
Original Victorian Neo-Byzantine gold and blue décor with a modern Italian/American menu.

L'Escargot
48 Greek Street, W1
020 7437 2679
www.lescargotrestaurant.co.uk
A Soho institution that has modernised itself but retains its reputation for quality.

French House Dining Room
49 Dean Street, WC2
020 7437 2477
Tiny restaurant with a modern British menu above the pub famous for its artist clientele.

Giovanni's
10 Goodwin's Court, St Martin's Lane, WC2
020 7240 2877
Classic Italian style food and atmosphere in an ultra discreet location.

Au Jardin des Gourmets
5 Greek Street, W1
020 7437 1816
Traditional French elegance with modern French cuisine.

RS Hispaniola
Victoria Embankment, WC2
020 7839 3011
www.hispaniola.co.uk
A restaurant ship offering a superb view of the Thames and a modern Mediterranean menu.

Kettners
29 Romilly Street, W1
020 7734 6112
www.kettners.com
Go upstairs for the real atmosphere as downstairs it's just a pizza place – there's a champagne bar if you want to push the boat out.

Luigi's
15 Tavistock Street, WC2
020 7240 1795
Gracious old school Italian atmosphere and food.

Mon Plaisir
21 Monmouth Street, WC2
020 7836 7243
www.monplaisir.co.uk
Family run French restaurant with intimate atmosphere and traditional cuisine.

Orso
27 Wellington Street, WC2
020 7240 5269
www.orsorestaurant.com
Joe Allen's more sophisticated elder brother serving modern Italian food.

Papageno
29-31 Wellington Street, WC2
020 7836 4444
Over the top Operatic Baroque atmosphere grill with live opera on Sunday and Monday nights.

Porters
17 Henrietta Street, WC2
020 7836 6466
www.porters.uk.com
Traditional English fare – pies a speciality.

Salieri
376 Strand, WC2
020 7836 1318
Highly theatrical décor, modern international cuisine – and a harpist.

Sarastro
126 Drury Lane, WC2B
020 7836 0101
www.sarastro-restaurant.com
Over the top Operatic Baroque atmosphere "the show after the show" and modern Mediterranean menu.

J Sheekey
28-32 St Martin's Court, WC2
020 7240 2565
www.j-sheekey.co.uk
Famous fish restaurant that has become fashionable amongst show folk.

Teatro
93-107 Shaftesbury Avenue, W1
020 7494 3040
www.teatrosoho.co.uk
Chic minimalist décor and modern menu have combined to create a current hot favourite.

Tiddy Dols
55 Shepherd Market, W1
020 7499 2357
18th century Mayfair house preserving its Hogarthian atmosphere offering traditional English fayre.

UPPER CIRCLE (ECONOMY)

Ed's Easy Diner
15 Great Newport Street, WC2
020 7836 0271
12 Moor Street, W1
020 7434 4439
19 Rupert Street, W1
020 7287 1951
www.edseasydiner.co.uk
American style 1950s diner with traditional menu.

Food For Thought
31 Neal Street, WC2
020 7836 9072
Homely veggie heaven with a change of menu daily.

Gaby's Deli
30 Charing Cross Road, WC2
020 7836 4233
London's authentic New York style deli diner.

Jimmy's Restaurant
23 Frith Street, W1
020 7437 9521
Old time Greek family café of the kind that doesn't exist any more.

Mildred's
58 Greek Street, W1
020 7494 1631
Friendly home cooking veggie cafe.

My Old Dutch
131 High Holborn, WC1
020 7242 5200
Dutch pancake house with gigantic plates (and pancakes).

Pasta Brown
31-32 Bedford Street, WC2
020 7836 7486
35-36 Bow Street, WC2
020 7379 5775
Modern no nonsense pasta cafes.

Pollo
20 Old Compton Street, W1
020 7734 5917
Simple Italian menu in substantial portions.

The Rock & Sole Plaice
47 Endell Street, WC2
020 7836 3785
A no frills great British fish and chip shop.

Steph's
39 Dean Street, W1
020 7734 5976
www.stephs-restaurant.com
Fun atmosphere and fun food

The Stockpot
18 Old Compton Street, W1
020 7287 1066
38 Panton Street, SW1
020 7839 5142
Very cheap and very cheerful English food

Wine Bars & Brasseries

The Archduke
Concert Hall Approach,
South Bank, SE1
020 7928 9370
Between the potted palms underneath the arches – *the* venue on
the South Bank.

Le Beaujolais
25 Litchfield Street, WC2
020 7836 2277
Popular simple unpretentious
French wine bar.

Café Boheme
13 Old Compton Street, W1
020 7734 0263
French classic wine and food – and
live jazz.

Le Café des Amis Du Vin
11-14 Hanover Place, WC2
020 7379 3444
Classic French wine bar with a
stylish modern makeover.

Conservatory Bar
15 St Giles High Street, WC2
020 7836 8956
Surprisingly good food and drink
in an unlikely setting – late music
on weekends.

Cork & Bottle
44-46 Cranbourn Street, WC2
020 7734 7807
Most Londoner's favourite – huge
wine list and great food in a usually heaving basement.

Crusting Pipe
27 The Market Covent Garden, WC2
020 7836 1415
Authentic Dickensian atmosphere
often mellowed by a string quartet.

Davy's at St James'
Crown Passage Vaults, 20 King Street, W1
020 7839 8831
A warren of former silver vaults
provides a uniquely intimate
environment.

Dover Street Wine Bar
8-10 Dover Street, W1
020 7491 7509
www.doverst.co.uk
As famous for its live jazz as its
wine and food.

The Fire Station
150 Waterloo Road, SE1
020 7620 2226
Former emergency services depot
transformed into a cavernous bar.

Garrick Wine Bar
10-12 Garrick Street, WC2
020 7240 7649
Sit upstairs and watch the comings
and goings at the famous club.

Gordon's Wine Bar
47 Villiers Street, WC2
020 7930 1408
www.gordonswinebar.com
Deliciously dark and dingy cel-
lar with open fire in winter and
summer terrace (Rudyard Kipling
lived here).

Grape Street Wine Bar
224A Shaftesbury Avenue, WC2
020 7240 0686
Bright modern and cheery and a
good selection.

Hamptons
15 Whitcomb Street, WC2
020 7839 2823
Plain and simple with a wide
selection – exactly what a wine bar
should be.

PJ's Grill
30 Wellington Street, WC2
020 7240 7529
www.pjsgrill.net
Old fashioned but handsome American style grill with a classic menu.

Da Marco
417 Strand, WC2
020 7836 0654
Narrow wood panelled rooms that
have an authentic Victorian air.

Randall & Aubin
16 Brewer Street, W1
020 7287 4447
Deli turned seafood/rotisserie bar.

Tuttons
11-12 Russell Street, WC2
020 7257 8613
www.tuttons.com
Choose indoors or out on the
Covent Garden Piazza.

Walkers Wine Bar
Craig's Court, 15 Whitehall, SW1
020 7925 0090
An entire house of bars with a
wide range of wines and ales.

The Anchor
34 Park Street, SE1
020 7407 1577
Reputedly Shakespeare's local in
Bankside lives up to expectation.

The Captain's Cabin
4 Norris Street, SW1
020 7930 4767
Formerly the Cock Tavern an 18th
century coaching inn.

Coach & Horses
29 Greek Street, W1
020 7437 5920
The setting of the play Jeffrey Bernard Is Unwell.

The Coal Hole
91 Strand, WC2
020 7836 7503
The basement bar appears not to
have changed in 100 years.

The Crown
51 New Oxford Street, WC1
020 7836 2752
Warm welcome inside in winter
and plenty of space outside under
the fairy lights in summer.

De Hems
11 Macclesfield Street, W1
020 7437 2494
Traditional Dutch hospitality –
popular with stage crew.

The French House
49 Dean Street, WC2
020 7437 2477
One of the most famous Soho locals - known for its artist clientele.

The George Inn
77 Borough High Street, SE1
020 7407 2056
Original 17th century coaching inn - supposedly where Nicholas Nickelby departed for Dotheboys Hall.

The Hand & Racquet
48 Whitcomb Street, SW1
020 7930 5905
The haunt of comic Tony Hancock and his writers Ray Galton and Alan Simpson who referred to it in their shows.

Kemble's Head
61 Long Acre, WC2
020 7836 4845
Named after Philip Kemble the manager of Covent Garden and Drury Lane with etchings of both.

The Lamb & Flag
32 Rose Street, WC2
020 7497 9504
Open since 1627 it claims to be central London's oldest tavern.

Lyceum Tavern
354 Strand, WC2
020 78367155
Oak panelled rooms suitable for Henry Irving who appears on its sign.

The Nag's Head
10 James Street, WC2
020 7836 4678
Hertfordshire ales and etchings of Covent Garden theatres - popular with Opera House staff.

Ye Old Cheshire Cheese
145 Fleet Street, EC4
020 7353 6170
The epitome of the Victorian city pub with genuine atmosphere.

Opera Tavern
23 Catherine Street, WC2
020 7636 7321
Traditional Victorian style - haunt of Drury Lane show cast members.

Old Bank of England
194 Fleet Street, EC4
020 7430 2255
Once the Law Courts branch of the Bank of England now spectacularly restored.

Punch & Judy
40 The Market Covent Garden, WC2
020 7379 0923
Named in honour of Britain's first puppet show presented under St Paul's portico opposite.

Roundhouse
1 Garrick Street, WC2
020 7836 9838
The haunt of theatregoers since 1868.

The Round Table
St Martin's Court, WC2
020 78366436
Authentic dark wood panelled rooms - popular with show crew.

The Salisbury
St Martin's Lane, WC2
London's greatest Victorian
pub and the most popular with
theatrefolk – featured in the film
Travels With My Aunt.

Sherlock Holmes
10 Northumberland Street, WC2
020 7930 2644
Full of Holmesian memora-
bilia with small museum upstairs
– unique sign has Holmes on one
side and Watson on the other.

Silver Cross
25-33 Whitehall, SW1
020 7930 8350
The site of an inn since 1867 it features much Victorian memorabilia.

The Ship & Shovell
1 & 3 Craven Passage, WC2
020 7838 1311
Two separate buildings on each
side of an alleyway

Three Greyhounds
25 Greek Street, W1
020 7287 0754
Eclectic Soho clientele create a
unique atmosphere.

Cafes & Tea Venues

ROYAL BOX (FIRST CLASS)

Brown's Hotel
Albemarle Street, W1
020 7493 6020
www.brownshotel.com
Step back in time to a Victorian
town house of great character.

Fortnum & Mason Soda Fountain
181 Piccadilly, W1
020 7734 8040
www.fortnumandmason.co.uk
A true London original inspired by
1950s America.

The Ritz Palm Court
150 Piccadilly, W1
020 7493 8181
www.theritzhotel.co.uk
A charming room with a view
across Green Park

Waldorf Hilton Palm Court
The Aldwych
020 7836 2400
www.hilton.co.uk/waldorf
Tea among the potted palms,
marble and mirrors – dances if you
desire.

DRESS CIRCLE (CLUB CLASS)

Museum Street Café
17 Museum Street, WC1
020 7405 3211
Upmarket foodie approach to tea-
time classics.

National Portrait Gallery Café
St Martin's Place, WC2
020 7312 2490
www.npg.org.uk
Offers views across the rooftops of
Trafalgar Square and Westminster.

Richoux
171 Piccadilly, W1
020 7493 2204
www.richoux.co.uk
A stylish continental coffee house.

St Martin-in-the-fields Café in the Crypt
5 St Martin's Place, Trafalgar Square, WC2
020 7766 1158
www.stmartin-in-the-fields.org
Cream cakes in the atmospheric brick arches beneath the famous church.

UPPER CIRCLE (ECONOMY)

Amalfi
29-31 Old Compton Street, W1
020 7437 7284
Simple Italian decor and sensational Italian cakes.

Bar Italia
22 Frith Street, W1
020 7437 4520
Preserves the '50s family run espresso coffee bar atmosphere.

Cappuccetto Patisserie
9-10 Moor Street, W1
020 7437 9472
Homely Italian cafe with terrific cakes.

Maison Bertaux
28 Greek Street, W1
020 7437 6007
Actress Michelle Wade, who started as a waitress and now owns the company, stages occasional performances upstairs.

Patisserie Valerie
44 Old Compton Street, W1
020 7437 3466
Retains its student café air despite being packed with showbiz types – and wonderful cakes.

Internet Cafés

EasyEverything
457-459 Strand, WC2
www.easyEverything.com
All the charm of a call centre but lots of terminals and open 24/7.

Mocha Cafe
61 Charing Cross Road, WC2
A pleasant patisserie with terminals at the rear.

Pizza Express
10 Dean Street, W1
020 7437 9595
www.pizzaexpresslive.co.uk
A special outlet of the chain
which features regular appearances
by world class jazz musicians.

Pizza On The Park
11 Knightsbridge, SW1
020 7235 7825
www.pizzaonthepark.co.uk
London's only remaining cabaret
room presenting a repertoire of
sophisticated entertainers.

Ronnie Scotts
47 Frith Street, W1
020 7439 0747
www.ronniescotts.co.uk
The premier jazz venue has had a
subtle makeover but continues as
before.

NO S
SILENC

FINALE -
THEATREGOERS LONDON

Finale • Theatregoers London

Tours

Make Your Own Theatreland Walking Tour

The tour starts and ends under the portico of **St Paul's Church (1)** in Covent Garden, where the opening scene of Shaw's *Pygmalion* – or Lerner and Loewe's *My Fair Lady* – takes place. An inscription records that Samuel Pepys saw the first Punch and Judy show in England here in 1662, hence the name of the pub in the Market building opposite. It is known as the actor's church as it contains plaques commemorating many theatrical figures, and memorial services are often held there.

As you make your way you will find that many of the streets in the Covent Garden area are named after actors and managers including Betterton, Garrick, Irving, Kean, Keeley, Kemble and Macklin.

Walk through the north aisle of the market building, passing Pollock's Toy Theatre shop on the left, to the north east corner of the piazza where there is now an entrance to the **Royal Opera House (2)**. The bookshop, and the café in the Floral Hall, originally the flower market, are open all day.

Exit at the front of the building in Bow Street. Turn right and walk down Bow Street. Turn left into Russell Street and on the left is the **Fortune (3)**.

On the right is the colonnade at the side of the **Theatre Royal Drury Lane (4)**. Cross over, walk back under the colonnade and turn left into Catherine Street. On the corner is a drinking fountain dedicated to Sir Augustus Harris, manager of Drury Lane in the late 19th century, who was nicknamed "Druriolanus". Just beyond is the famous portico with the royal crest.

Continue down Catherine Street and on the right is the **Duchess (5)**. On the left, just opposite, is the **Novello (6)**.

Turn left into Aldwych. Above the door to the right of the theatre, at number 11 is a blue plaque marking the entrance to the flat where composer and performer Ivor Novello lived, and which is now a theatre producer's office. Walk past the Waldorf Hilton (or pop in for a Tea Dance) and at the other end of the block is the **Aldwych (7)**. Opposite and just ahead you will see Bush House, home of BBC World Service radio.

Retrace your steps to the end of Catherine Street, continue to the end of Aldwych and turn right into the Strand, as in the music hall song "Let's all go down the Strand". On your right in Wellington Street is another famous portico, that of the **Lyceum (8)**. In the Strand the first turning on the left is Savoy Street, off which is Savoy Hill where the BBC's – and the world's – first radio studios were located.

Continue along the Strand, and on the left in Savoy Court, the entrance to the Savoy Hotel, is the **Savoy (9)**. Only the box office is above ground level here as it is on a steeply sloping site – the original entrance was on the Embankment.

Almost opposite on the right is Southampton Street where on the left above the door at number 27 is a bronze plaque with a bas-relief profile commemorating where actor manager David Garrick lived. Further along the Strand on the right is the **Vaudeville (10)**, and the **Adelphi (11)**.

Continue along the Strand until you reach Charing Cross station. Turn left into Villiers Street and then right into The Arches under the station – as in the song "Underneath The Arches I dream my dreams away". Here on the left is the **New Players Theatre (12)**, where Sandy Wilson's show *The Boy Friend* was first presented. Emerging from the The Arches you pass between the two halves of the Ship and Shovel pub.

At the end of the alleyway turn left into Craven Street, and at the bottom on the left is the **Playhouse (13)**.

Make a U-turn to the right into Northumberland Avenue, and then turn left into Great Scotland Yard, the original home of the Metropolitan Police. At the end turn right into Whitehall and on your left are the **Trafalgar Studios (14)**. To its left is Horse Guards Parade where yet another kind of theatre, The Changing Of The Guard, takes place.

Continue along Whitehall northwards, skirt the eastern side of Trafalgar Square, past St Martin-in-the-Fields church on the right, where free lunchtime recitals are held, into St Martin's Lane, noting the animated figure of a barrel maker above The Chandos pub on the corner. On the right is the **London Coliseum (15)**. This is a London landmark because it is surmounted by a tower with a revolving globe on top.

Almost opposite is the **Duke of York's (16)**. Further up on the left is Cecil Court, an alleyway where there are a number of theatrical ephemera shops.

Keep going and also on the left is the great genuine Victorian theatre pub The Salisbury, next door to the **Noël Coward (17)**.

A little further on you come to a junction of five streets. To the right is Garrick Street, where the Garrick Club, the famous gentleman's club which has counted many actors amongst its members, is located at number 15 – a rather dowdy building on the right. Ignoring that, and with only a glance ahead to the right at Stringfellow's, take the second exit to the left, Great Newport Street and on the right is the **Arts (18)**.

At the end of this short street turn left into Charing Cross Road, passing on your right the Cirque, built to stage circus and water spectaculars but now a nightclub. On your left is the **Wyndham's (19)**, and further on, also on the left is the **Garrick (20)**.

Cross over the road and you will find an imposing statue of Sir Henry Irving, the first actor to be knighted in 1895, standing on a large plinth in a small garden backing on to the rear of the National Portrait Gallery, at the junction of Irving Street. The gallery houses portraits of many theatrical figures. Walk along Irving Street into the south side of Leicester Square and on your right is the **tkts-Official half Price Ticket Booth (21)** located in the clock tower pavilion.

Skirt round the western side of Leicester Square, noting the statue of William Shakespeare, which forms the centrepiece to the fountain in the middle of the garden, and the hand prints of actors in the footpath next to the railings. Turn left into New Coventry Street. Continue ahead and on the left is the **Prince of Wales (22)**.

Turn left into Oxendon Street, where The Comedy Store, the British national theatre of comedy, is on the right. At the next corner is the **Comedy (23)**. Turn right into Panton Street and then left into Haymarket, and on the left is the Nash portico of the **Theatre Royal Haymarket (24)** with its royal crest over the entrance. Cross over the road and opposite is **Her Majesty's (25),** where there is a bronze plaque commemorating actor manager Herbert Beerbohm Tree, its builder. At the rear of the theatre is the Royal Opera Arcade, all that remains of the additions made to the earlier theatre by Nash in 1818.

Walk back up Haymarket to the top, and turn left into Piccadilly Circus. On the left is the London Pavilion, once a great music hall, where Marie Lloyd sang *"the boy I love is up in the gallery"*, but now sadly reduced to a shopping centre. On the left is the **Criterion (26)**, almost opposite another

London icon, the Shaftesbury Memorial – the statue popularly known as Eros. The view up Shaftesbury Avenue from here is the image that usually represents London Theatre, as Times Square does Broadway. Misplaced good taste has decreed that Piccadilly Circus can no longer compare with the neon lights of Times Square as they are now restricted to just one building.

Take the forth exit to the left Glasshouse Street, almost immediately forking right into Sherwood Street and on your right is the **Piccadilly (27)**.

Turn right into Denman Street at the end of which on the left in Great Windmill Street is the Windmill Theatre. Its motto "we never closed" – referring to the fact that it continued to play throughout World War II – was often corrupted to "we never clothed" as it presented non-stop revue, with a programme which alternated nude tableaux and comedians. Although there have been ordinary shows staged there, it has returned to its origins and is now a table dancing establishment. Turn left into Shaftesbury Avenue, and on your right is the Trocadero, another music hall now reduced to a shopping centre.

This is the heart of London's Theatreland with the **Lyric (28)** and the **Apollo (29)** next door to each other and the **Gielgud (30)** and the **Queen's (31)** forming the ends of the next block. At the time of writing major building works are a being undertaken to extend the Gielgud and Queen's and to include a new theatre – the Sondheim – above the Queen's.

Continue up Shaftesbury Avenue to Cambridge Circus and on the left is the **Palace (32)**, another London landmark.

Turn left at the side of the theatre into Romilly Street and on the next corner on the right is the Coach & Horses, the pub that is the setting for the play Jeffrey Bernard Is Unwell. Norman Balon 'the rudest landlord in London', has recently retired and service at the establishment may regrettably have improved. Turn right into Greek Street and on the next corner on the left is the **Prince Edward (33)**.

Turn right into Old Compton Street and then left into Charing Cross Road, and on the right is the **Phoenix (34)**. Opposite is the famous Foyles bookshop, which is one of London's largest. Continue up to St Giles Circus, passing on the right the monument to 1960s property speculation, Centre Point which remained unoccupied for 20 years. Looking left into Oxford Street, The Tottenham pub is on the site of Oxford Music Hall. Ahead on the right is the **Dominion (35)**.

Turn right into New Oxford Street and immediately right again into St Giles High Street, passing on the right St Giles-in-the-Fields, another church which has seen many theatrical memorial services. Continue on, crossing the upper part of Shaftesbury Avenue, and on the left is the **Shaftesbury (36)**. Public outcry at plans to demolish it after the run of Hair was brought to an end by the ceiling falling in, organised by Save London's Theatre Campaign, led to the founding of The Theatres Trust to protect endangered theatres.

Retrace your steps to Shaftesbury Avenue, turn left and walk back towards Cambridge Circus, passing the Odeon cinema on your right. This was formerly the Saville theatre, and again an outcry was caused when it was converted to twin cinemas without any notice in 1970. It was the last West End theatre to be lost to live performance.

Just before Cambridge Circus on the right is Angels the premier British costumier. Turn left into West Street almost opposite and on the left are the **Ambassadors (37)** and **St Martin's (38)**. *The Mousetrap*, the world's longest running play, opened at the first and then transferred to the second. Opposite is The Ivy, the restaurant with great theatrical connections – London's equivalent to Sardi's (if such a thing could exist).

At the end of West Street turn left into Monmouth Street, pausing to see if any stars emerge from the building on the corner, which houses the actors union Equity. Walk up, passing Dress Circle, London's greatest showbiz record and bookshop on the right, to Seven Dials, where the **Cambridge (39)** is on the right.

Take Earlham Street, which runs along its left side, and the **Donmar Warehouse (40)**, one of London's most innovative theatres is on the left.

At the end of Earlham Street turn right into Neal Street. Continue straight ahead, crossing Long Acre, and at the end of James Street is Covent Garden. This is where you started at **St Paul's Church (1)**.

Conducted Walking Tours

These usually last about two hours and take place all year round regardless of the weather.

And Did Those Feet...
Guided Walks
249 Evering Road, E5 8AL
Tel: 020 8806 4325
www.chr.org.uk/cswalks.htm
Guided walks tracing the history of theatre in London and exploring two cultural quarters in depth.

Ghosts Of The West End
Original London Walks
PO Box 1708, London, NW6 4LW
Tel: 020 7624 3978
www.walks.com
Visit the gaslight alleyways – plus over 100 other walks in mornings, afternoons and evenings every day.

The London Of Dickens And Shakespeare Historical Tours
3 Florence Road,
South Croydon, CR2 0PQ
Tel: 020 8668 5327
Southwark and Bankside on Sunday mornings plus others.

The Shakespeare City Walk
City Secrets Walks,
31 Dibdin House, London, W9 1QE
Tel: 020 7625 5155
www.shakespeareguide.com
Walk where the Bard worked and played.

Sweet Love Remember'd
Shakespeare's Globe Theatre
Celebrates Shakespeare's birthday on 23rd April by walks starting in Westminster or Shoreditch with 12 sonneteers entertaining along a route through Tudor London.

Theatreland Walking Tours
Society Of London Theatre
Tel: 020 7557 6700
www.officiallondontheatre.co.uk
Visit the West End's most historic theatres monthly on Sunday afternoons on the official tour, which includes tea and a map.

Self Guided Audio Tours

Footnotes Audio Walks
112 Rodenhurst Road SW4 8AP
Tel: 020 8671 0597
www.footnotesaudiowalks.co.uk
The only self guided walking tour of London theatreland on CD, tape or MP3 download

Backstage Tours

These take place at the following theatres:
Barbican Centre
Drury Lane
Haymarket
London Coliseum
London Palladium
Prince Edward
Prince of Wales
New London
Royal Albert Hall
Royal Court
Royal National Theatre
Royal Opera House
Sadler's Wells
Shakespeare's Globe

The Theatrical Calendar

January

New Year's Day London Parade
Research House, Fraser Road,
Greenford, Middlesex, UB6 7AQ
Tel: 020 8566 8586
Recorded information hotline:
0900 525 2001 (UK only)
www.londonparade.co.uk
Marching bands and floats parade
around the West End.

Twelfth Night Celebrations (6th)
Shakespeare's Globe,
New Globe Walk, SE1 9DT
The arrival of the Holly Man her-
alds a Mummers Play, distribution
of 'Orr Cakes, and a procession to
the George Inn.

London International Mime
Festival
35 Little Russell Street, WC1A 2HH
Tel: 020 7637 5661
www.mimefest.co.uk
Presenting visual theatre, mime,
circus, puppetry and clowning
from around the world.

Get Into London Theatre
Society Of London Theatre
www.getintolondontheatre.com
Discounted tickets designed to
encourage new and young theatregoers.

February

Chinese New Year
Gerrard Street/Wardour Street, W1
Chinatown celebrates with lion
dancing, fire crackers and food.

Joseph Grimaldi
Memorial Service (first Sunday)
Holy Trinity, Beechwood Road,
Dalston E8 4EZ
Tel: 0870 128 4335
www.clowns-international.co.uk
A unique service attended by
clowns held at the Clown's
Church in Hackney.

The Laurence Olivier Awards
Society Of London Theatre
www.olivierawards.co.uk
Britain's premier theatre awards.

April

Chaucer Festival
Southwark Cathedral,
London Bridge, SE1 9DA
Tel: 020 7229 0635
Costumed procession to the Tower
of London for a medieval Fayre
celebrating

Shakespeare's Birthday (23rd)
Shakespeare's Globe,
New Globe Walk, SE1 9DT
Programme of celebrations and ac-
companied Sonnet Walks through
the city.

May

May Fayre & Puppet Festival
St Paul's Church Covent Garden,
WC2E 9ED
Tel: 020 7375 0441
Commemorates Punch and Judy's
first appearance in Britain under
the portico in 1662

Museums & Galleries Month
Tel:020 7233 6789
www.museumsweek.org.uk
Special events at museums and
galleries.

Evening Standard Awards
Northcliffe House,
2 Derry Street, W8 5TT
Tel: 020 7938 6000
www.thisislondon.com
London's own theatre awards.

Chelsea Festival
The Crypt, St Luke's Church,
Sydney Street, SW3 6NH
Tel: 020 7349 8101
www.chelseafestival.org.uk
Opera and music events around
the Royal Borough.

City of London Festival
Bishopsgate Hall,
230 Bishopsgate, EC2M 4HW
Tel: 020 7377 0540
www.colf.org
Presents a diverse range of art
forms in splendid City buildings.

West End Live (third weekend)
Leicester Square
www.westendlive.co.uk
A two day programme of live
performances by artists from West
End shows.

June

Spitalfields Festival
75 Brushfield Street, E1 6AA
Tel: 020 7377 0287
www.spitalfieldsfestival.org.uk
Classical music in a striking baroque church.

**London International Festival Of
Theatre**
19-20 Great Sutton Street,
EC1V 0DR
Tel: 020 7863 8017
www.liftfest.org.uk
Presenting cutting edge theatre
companies from all over the world.

July

Almeida Opera Festival
Almeida Theatre, Almeida Street,
Islington, N1 1TA
Presenting contemporary opera
and music events.

The BBC Proms (to September)
Box Office, Royal Albert Hall,
Kensington Gore, SW7 2AP
Tel: 020 7589 8212
www.bbc.co.uk/radio3/proms
The world's greatest classical music
festival.

Midsomer Village Fayre
(second Sunday)
St Paul's Church Covent Garden,
WC2E 9ED
Tel: 020 7375 0441
A traditional summer fete with
celebrities in attendance in the
churchyard.

Greenwich And Docklands Festival
Greenwich and Docklands
www.festival.org
Outdoor music, dance, theatre and
puppetry events.

August

Kids Week
Society Of London Theatre
www.kidsweek.co.uk
Children go free to West End
shows with paying adults.

Notting Hill Carnival
(last weekend)
Ladbroke Grove, W10
Europe's biggest street festival.

September

London Open House
(third weekend)
PO Box 25361, London, NW5 1GY
www.londonopenhouse.org
Offers access to normally private
buildings of architectural interest
usually including backstage tours.

Thames Festival
(third weekend)
The Bargehouse, Oxo Tower Wharf,
South Bank, SE1 9PH
Tel: 020 7928 8998
www.thamesfestival.org
Family activities, street theatre,
music and events along the river
and in the streets and parks nearby.

October

Dance Umbrella
20 Chancellors Street, W6 9RN
Tel: 020 8741 4040
www.danceumbrella.co.uk
Presenting the best of national and
international contemporary dance.

Pick Of The Fringe
1 Lumley Court, Off 402 Strand,
WC2H 0NB
Tel 0845 434 9290
Winners and nominees of the Ed-
inburgh Festival Fringe Comedy
awards play the West End.

November

Lord Mayor's Show
(second Saturday morning)
www.lordmayorsshow.org
Marching bands and floats parade
around the City of London.

December

Spitalfields Winter Festival
www.spitalfieldsfestival.org.uk
Christmas music by candlelight in
a striking baroque church.

Alternatives to the Show

Bateaux London
Embankment Pier, Victoria Embankment, WC2N
Tel: 020 7695 1800
www.bateauxlondon.com
Evening dinner and dance and Sunday lunch jazz cruises down the Thames.

Comedy Store
Haymarket House, Oxenden Street, WC2
Tel: 020 7344 4444
www.thecomedystore.co.uk
Britain's National Theatre of comedy – late night shows on weekends.

Holland Park Theatre
Holland Park, W8
Tel: 020 7602 7856
Open air opera performances June – August.

House Of Magic
Tel: 020 7735 3434
www.houseofmagic.co.uk
An entire enchanted house is the spectacular setting for a show of baffling illusions. At a secret location in central London.

ICA - (Institute of Contemporary Arts)
The Mall, SW1
Tel: 020 7930 3647
www.ica.org.uk
Performance art at its most esoteric.

Jongleurs
Central booking 0870 787 0707
Locations:
Bow Wharf, 221 Grove Road, E3
Camden Lock, 211-216 Chalk Farm Road, NW1
Battersea, 49 Lavender Gardens, SW11
www.jongleurs.com
Nationwide chain of comedy clubs has three branches in London.

Kenwood Concerts
Kenwood House Hampstead Lane, NW3
Tel: Booking 0870 890 0146
www.picnicconcerts.com
Open air classical concerts by the lake in July and August. The 2007 season was cancelled due to substantial losses in the previous year which was apparently caused by council restrictions on the number of events in response to noise complaints by local residents. Check the website to find out when and if the concerts will return.

London Showboat
Westminster Pier, SW1
Tel: 020 7740 0400
www.citycruises.com/showboat.htm
Cabaret and dinner as you cruise down the Thames past the sights of London.

Magic Circle
12 Stephenson Way, NW1
Tel: 020 7387 2222
www.themagiccircle.co.uk
Regular public shows and tours of the home of British magicians.

Medieval Banquet
The Beefeater, Ivory House, St Katherine's Dock, E1
Tel. 020 7480 5353
www.medievalbanquet.com
Join Henry VIII for a medieval banquet and entertainment experience.

Murder Mystery Dinner Theatre
New Connaught Rooms, 61-63 Great Queen Street, WC2
Tel: 020 7404 4232
www.murderevents.co.uk
Solve a crime as you eat dinner in a central London hotel.

The Players' Theatre Company
12 Bentinck Mansions, Bentinck Street, W1U 2ER
Tel: 020 7839 1134
www.playerstheatre.co.uk
Monthly Victorian Music Hall performances at different venues.

Free Entertainment and Events

Theatre

Laurence Olivier Awards

Each autumn the Society Of London Theatre selects fourteen enthusiastic and knowledgeable theatregoers to join one of the four judging panels for Britain's premier theatre awards – the Laurence Olivier Awards. Panelists receive a pair of free tickets for all shows playing in the West End during the following calendar year. Members of the Theatre panel are expected to attend about 60 play or 20 musical performances, Dance about 40, and Opera and Affiliates (visiting shows in Off West End venues) about 20 each. Applications can be made online on the SOLT web site, or by filling out the form in the leaflets to be found in all West End theatres.

Kids Week in the West End

Children go free to West End shows with paying adults during the last two weeks in August. Organised by the Society Of London Theatre.

National Theatre

An extensive programme of events ranging from foyer music to platform productions and discussions, some requiring booking and payment. Ask the Box Office for details of the night you are attending when you make your reservation. In addition there is the Watch This Space festival of out-door events in Theatre Square during the summer months.

Theatre Royal Haymarket Masterclass

A programme of afternoon masterclasses with actors, directors and writers for 17 to 30 year olds who have an interest in theatre, or are keen to pursue a career in the arts, plus workshops focussing on particular techniques.

Royal Opera House

Live relays of opera and ballet performances on a giant screen in the Covent Garden Piazza and other locations during the summer months. Chamber music concerts in the Linbury Theatre on Mondays at 1.00pm.

Concerts

Concert Venues

Barbican Centre
Foyer music weekdays from 5.30pm and Sundays from 12.30pm, plus ad hoc talks, workshops and family events on Sundays related to current season. Again check with the Box Office for details.

LSO St Luke's
Concerts on Fridays at 1pm, plus open rehearsals by the London Symphony Orchestra at various times.

Royal Albert Hall BBC Proms
A series of fringe events including poetry, lectures, talks and conversations with composers accompany the main concert programme each summer.

Royal Festival Hall
Foyer music of all kinds Wednesdays to Sundays from 12.30pm, jazz on Fridays from 5.15pm, plus outdoor events on the terraces in the summer months.

Churches
Many churches hold lunchtime recitals on different days of the week.

The Grosvenor Chapel
South Audley Street, W1K 2PA
Tel: 020 7499 1684
Concerts on Tuesdays at 1.10pm

St Anne's Lutheran Church
Gresham Street, EC2V 7BX
Tel: 020 7606 4986
Concerts on Mondays and Fridays at 1.10pm.

St George's Cathedral Southwark
Westminster Bridge Road, SE1 7HY
Tel: 020 7933 5256
Organ and other recitals on Fridays (& occasional Saturdays) at 1.05pm.

St Giles-in-the Fields
60 St Giles High Street, WC2H 8LG
Tel: 020 7240 2532
Spring and autumn seasons of recitals on Fridays at 1.10pm, plus occasional pre dinner concerts.

St James's Piccadilly
197 Piccadilly, W1J 9LL
Tel: 020 7734 4511
Recitals on Mondays, Wednesdays and Fridays at 1.10pm.

St John's Waterloo
Waterloo Road, SE1 8TY
Tel: 020 7633 9819
St Martin-in-the Fields
Concerts on Wednesdays at 1.10pm.

Finale • Free Entertainment & Events

St Martin-in-the Fields
Trafalgar Square, WC2N 4JJ
Tel: 020 7839 8362
Concerts on Mondays, Tuesdays
and Fridays at 1.05pm.

St Mary le Bow
Cheapside, EC2V 6AU
Tel: 020 7248 5139
Concerts on Thursdays at 1.05pm.

St Pancras Parish Church
Euston Road, NW1 2BA
Tel: 020 7388 1461
Recitals Thursdays at 1.15pm.

St Paul's Cathedral
St Paul's Churchyard, EC4M 8AD
Tel: 020 7246 8357
Organ recitals on Sundays at 5pm,
and choral recitals on certain
weekdays at 1.15pm.

Southwark Cathedral
London Bridge, SE1 9DA
Tel: 020 7367 6700
Organ and other recitals on Mon-
days and Tuesdays at 1.10pm.

Temple Church
Temple, EC4Y 7BB
Tel: 020 7353 8559
Organ recitals on Wednesdays
at 1.15pm.

Westminster Abbey
Broad Sanctuary, SW1P 3PA
Tel: 020 7654 4900
Organ recitals on Sundays at
5.45pm, and band concerts in
College Garden on Thursdays at
12.30pm in the summer months.

Colleges
The main music colleges present a
programme of lunchtime and evening concerts with a wide variety
of music during term time.

Guildhall School of Music & Drama
Royal Academy of Music
Royal College of Music
Trinity College of Music

TV & Radio
Free tickets are available for
recordings of radio and television
programmes from the BBC
and independent production
companies.

Applause Store
Elstree Film & Television Studios,
Shenley Road, Borehamwood,
Hertfordshire, WD6 1JG
Tel: 08700 24 1000
www.applausestore.com

BBC TV & Radio Shows
BBC Audience Services, PO Box
3000, BBC TV Centre, W12 7RJ
Tel: 020 8576 1227
Information Hot Line: 020 7765 5858
www.bbc.co.uk/tickets

Beonscreen
Cecil Road, Kingswood,
Bristol, BS15 8NA
Tel: 08700 632932
www.beonscreen.com/uk

Clappers
86 Malford Grove,
South Woodford, E18 2DY
Tel: 020 8532 2771 / 020 8532 2770
www.clappers-tickets.co.uk

Hat Trick Productions
10 Livonia Street, W1V 3PH
Ticket Unit Tel: 020 7287 1598
www.hattrick.com

Lost In TV
PO BOX 28791, E18 1YA
Tel: 020 8530 8100
www.lostintv.com

Powerhouse Film & TV
3 Bedfordbury, Covent Garden,
WC2N 4BP
Tel: 020 7240 2828

Standing Room Only Audiences
Tel: 020 8684 3333
www.sroaudiences.com

TV Recordings
Avalon Television,
4A Exmoor Street, W10 6BD
Tel: 020 7598 5000
www.tvrecordings.com

Places Of Theatrical Interest

Museums, Exhibitions & Research Facilities

Barbican Performing Arts & Music Library - Music Performance Research Centre
Barbican Centre,
Silk Street, EC2 8DS
Library Tel: 020 7638 0672

Jerwood Library of Performing Arts
Trinity College of Music,
Old Royal Naval College,
Greenwich, SE10 9JF
Tel: 020 8305 3951

Music Performance Research Centre
www.musicpreserved.org
Performing arts books, scores and recordings of live performance and interviews.

British Library - National Sound Archive
96 Euston Road, NW1 2DB
Tel: Library 020 7412 7332
Tel: National Sound Archive
020 7412 7676
Tel: Dept of Manuscript 020 7412 7513
www.bl.uk
Department of Manuscripts holds scripts submitted to Lord Chamberlain's office for licensing plus playbills and theatre notices and National Sound Archive contains recordings of performance and interviews.

Dulwich College Archives
Dulwich, SE21 7LD
Tel: 020 8299 9201
www.dulwich.org.uk
Contain 11,000 books, diaries, account books and correspondence of its founder, the actor Edward Alleyn, and actor manager Phillip Henslow (both contemporaries of Shakespeare) and manuscripts and letters of P G Wodehouse.

The Raymond Mander & Joe Mitchenson Theatre Collection
Jerwood Library of the Performing Arts, Trinity College of Music,
Old Royal Naval College,
Greenwich, SE10 9JF
Tel: 020 8305 4426
www.mander-and-mitchenson.co.uk
A cornucopia of theatrical ephemera.

Museum of London
150 London Wall, EC2V 5HN
Tel: 0870 444 3852
www.museumoflondon.org.uk
Traces the history of London including entertainment.

National Art Library
Victoria and Albert Museum,
Cromwell Road, SW7 2RL
Tel: 020 7942 2400
www.vam.ac.uk/nal
First folios of plays by Shakespeare, Beaumont and Fletcher and Webster, exhibitions and talks.

National Portrait Gallery
St Martin's Place, WC2H OHE
Tel: 020 7306 0055
www.npg.org.uk
The collection includes paintings, photographs and busts of many performers and writers.

Pollocks Toy Theatre Museum
1 Scala Street, W1P 1LT
Tel: 020 7636 3452
www.pollocksmuseum.co.uk
Original toy theatres and models on display and also on sale.

The Rose Theatre
56 Park Street, SE1 9AR
Tel: 020 7593 0026
www.rosetheatre.org.uk
A light and sound presentation at the archaeological site of Bankside's first theatre.

Shakespeare's Globe Exhibition
New Globe Walk, Bankside, SE1 9DT
Tel: 020 7902 1500
www.shakespeares-globe.org
The most comprehensive exhibition about theatre in the time of Shakespeare.

Westminster Central Reference Library
35 St Martin's Street, WC2H 7HN
Tel: 020 7641 1300
Comprehensive collection of theatre and performing arts books.

Westminster Music Library
160 Buckingham Palace Road, SW1W 9TR
Tel: 020 7641 1300
Comprehensive collection of scores and music books.

Churches

St Martin-in-the-Fields
5 St Martin's Place, Trafalgar Square, WC2N 4JH
Tel: 020 7839 8362
www.stmartin-in-the-fields.org
Playwright George Farquhar and Nell Gwynne are amongst those buried here.

St Paul's Covent Garden
Bedford Street, WC2E 9ED
Tel: 020 7836 5221
Contains memorial plaques to many theatrical figures, some include a quotation from their best known role.

St Paul's Cathedral
Ludgate Hill, EC4M 8AE
Tel: 020 7246 8348
www.stpauls.co.uk
Arthur Sullivan and many musicians are buried here and there is a memorial to Ivor Novello.

Southwark Cathedral
London Bridge, SE1 9DA
Tel: 020 7367 6700
Shakespeare memorial with a reclining statue and stained glass window, his brother Edmund is buried here.

Westminster Abbey
Broad Sanctuary, SW1P 3PA
Tel: 020 7654 4900
www.westminster-abbey.org
Poet's Corner and the resting place of many writers including Chaucer, Sheridan, Dickens and Garrick's grave at the foot of the Shakespeare memorial.

Statues & Monuments

W S Gilbert - librettist
A memorial on the wall of the Embankment opposite Embankment Underground station.

Augustus Harris - manager of Drury Lane nicknamed 'Druriolanus'
A drinking fountain on the Catherine Street/Russell Street corner of the theatre.

Henry Irving - actor manager
A statue at the junction of Charing Cross Road and Irving Street WC2

J M Barrie - playwright
A statue of Peter Pan in Kensington Gardens W2 on the west bank of the Long Water.

Richard D'Oyly Carte - impresario who presented Gilbert and Sullivan operas
A sun dial in Embankment Gardens WC2 at the exit to Carting Lane.

David Garrick - actor manager
A bronze plaque with a bas-relief profile at 27 Southampton Street WC2

William Shakespeare - playwright
A statue forming the centre of a fountain in Leicester Square WC2.

Arthur Sullivan - composer
A bust above a figure representing music in mourning in Embankment Gardens WC2
on the corner of Savoy Place.

Herbert Beerbohm Tree - actor manager
A bronze plaque on Her Majesty's Theatre which he built.

Oscar Wilde - playwright
'A Conversation With Oscar Wilde' seat incorporating a bust in Adelaide Street WC2.

HENRY·IRVING
ACTOR

BORN·1838·DIED·1905·KNIGHT·LITT·D·DUBLIN·D·LITT
CAMBRIDGE·LL·D·GLASGOW·ERECTED·BY·ENGLISH
ACTORS·AND·ACTRESSES·AND·BY·OTHERS
CONNECTED·WITH·THE·THEATRE·IN·THIS·COUNTRY

Blue Plaques

John Logie Baird – inventor of television
22 Frith Street, W1 (site of the first transmission in 1926)
132-5 Long Acre, WC2

J M Barrie - playwright, novelist and poet
100 Bayswater Road, W2

Jack Buchanan - actor, dancer and manager
44 Mount Street, W1

Frances Hodgson Burnett - writer
63 Portland Place, W1

Arthur Conan Doyle - writer
2 Upper Wimpole Street, W1

Emma Cons - founder of the Old Vic
136 Seymour Place, W1

Charles Dickens - writer
48 Doughty Street, WC1

John Dryden - poet and playwright
43 Gerrard Street, W1

Edith Evans - actress
109 Ebury Street, SW1

John Galsworthy - writer
1-3 Robert Street, WC2

Nell Gwynne - actress
79 Pall Mall, SW1

George Frederick Handel - musician
25 Brook Street, W1

William Hazlett - essayist and theatre commentator
6 Frith Street, W1

Henry Irving - actor and manager
15A Grafton Street, W1

In a
on t
in l
WOLFGAN
MO
175
lived.
co
Royal Musi

Rudyard Kipling - poet and writer
43 Villiers Street, WC2

Lillie Langtry - actress
Cadogan Hotel, 22 Pont Street, SW1

Charles Laughton - actor
15 Percy Street, W1

Vivien Leigh - actress
54 Eaton Square, SW1

William Somerset Maugham - writer
6 Chesterfield Street, W1

Wolfgang Amadeus Mozart – composer
20 Frith Street, W1

Ivor Novello - composer and performer
11 The Aldwych, WC2

Arthur Wing Pinero - playwright
115A Harley Street, W1

George Bernard Shaw - playwright
29 Fitzroy Square, W1 (Side wall of the Lyric Theatre), Great Windmill Street, W1

Percy Bysshe Shelley - poet and playwright
15 Poland Street, W1

Richard Brinsley Sheridan - playwright and manager
14 Saville Row, W1

Marie Tempest - actress
24 Park Crescent, W1

Oscar Wilde - writer
34 Tite Street, SW3
Rear of Theatre Royal Haymarket, Suffolk Street, SW1

P.G. Wodehouse - writer
17 Dunraven Street, W1

website: www.english-heritage.org.uk/server/show/nav.1494

Theatre Shops

Books

Foyles
113-119 Charing Cross Road,
WC2H oEB
Tel: 020 7437 5660
www.foyles.co.uk

French's Theatre Book Shop
52 Fitzroy Street, W1P 6JR
Tel: 020 7387 9373
www.samuelfrench-london.co.uk

National Theatre Bookshop
Upper Ground, SE1 9PX
Tel: 020 7452 3456

**Offstage Theatre and
Film Bookshop**
34 Tavistock Street, WC2E 7PB
Tel: 020 7240 3883
www.offstagebooks.com

Royal Court Theatre Bookshop
Sloane Square, SW1
Tel: 020 7565 5024

Records, CDs & Music

Argent Zwemmer Printed Music
20 Denmark Street, WC2 H 8NA
Tel: 020 7379 3384

Boosey & Hawkes@Brittens
16 Wigmore Street, W1U 2RF
Tel: 0207 079 5940
www.boosey.com

**Chappell of Bond Street (also
instruments and publishers)**
152-160 Wardour Street, W1F 8YA
Tel: 020 7432 4400
www.chappellofbondstreet.co.uk

Dress Circle (also books)
*57-59 Monmouth Street, Upper St
Martin's Lane, WC2H 9DG*
Tel: 020 7240 2227
www.dresscircle.co.uk

First Night Records
2 Fitzroy Mews, W1P 5QD
Tel: 020 7383 7767
www.first-night-records.com

**Music Discount Centre
Opera Shop**
33 St Martin's Lane, WC2N 4ER
Tel/Fax: 020 7240 0270

Music Shop
Royal Festival Hall, SE1 8XX
Tel/Fax: 020 7620 0198
www.mdcmusic.co.uk

Rare Discs
*18 Bloomsbury Street, London,
WC1B 3QA*
Tel: 020 7580 3516

Royal Opera House Shop
Covent Garden, WC2E 9DD
Tel: 202 7212 9331

Travis & Emery
17 Cecil Court, WC2N 4EZ
Tel: 020 7240 2129

Memorabilia

David Drummond Pleasures Of Past Times (Victorian posters, post cards and books)
11 Cecil Court, WC2N 4EZ
Tel: 020 7836 1142

Pollocks Toy Theatres (Victorian model theatres)
Covent Garden Market, WC2E 8HA
Tel: 020 7379 7866
www.pollocks-coventgarden.co.uk

The Witchball (prints, posters and programmes)
2 Cecil Court, WC2N 4HE
Tel/Fax: 020 7836 2922

Vintage Magazine Shop
39 Brewer Street, W1R 3FD
Tel: 020 7439 8525
www.vinmag.com

Costume

Academy Costumes
50 Rushworth Street, SE1 0RB
Tel: 020 7620 0771
www.academycostumes.co.uk

Angels
119 Shaftesbury Avenue, WC2H 8AE
Tel: 020 7836 5678
www.fancydress.com

Cosprop
469 - 475 Holloway Road, N7 6LE
Tel: 020 7485 6999
www.cosprop.co.uk

Dancewear & Shoes

Anello & Davide
15 St Albans Grove,
Kensington, W8 5BP
Tel : 020 7938 2255
www.handmadeshoes.co.uk

Dancia International
187 Drury Lane, WC2B 5QD
Tel/Fax: 020 7831 9483
www.dancia.co.uk

Freed of London
94 St Martin's Lane, WC2N 4AT
Tel: 020 7240 0432
www.freedoflondon.com

Gamba Theatrical
Unit 14, Chingford Industrial Centre,
Hall Lane, E4 8DJ
Tel: 020 8529 9195

Porselli
9 West Street, WC2H 9NE
Tel: 020 7836 2862
www.porselli.co.uk

Make up & Wigs

Banbury Postiche
Little Bourton House, Southam
Road, Banbury,
Oxfordshire, OX16 1SR
Tel: 01295 757400
www.banburypostiche.co.uk

Charles H Fox
22 Tavistock Street, WC2E 7PY
Tel: 0870 2000 369
www.charlesfox.co.uk

Wig Specialities
173 Seymour Place, W1H 5TP
Tel: 020 7262 6565
www.wigspecialities.com

Musical Instruments

Ray Man (eastern)
54 Chalk Farm Road, NW1 8AN
Tel/Fax: 020 7692 6261

Macari's (guitars and electric)
92 Charing Cross Road,
WC2H 0JA
Tel: 020 7836 2856
www.macaris.co.uk

Paxman (brass)
Linton House, 164 Union Street,
SE1 0LH
Tel: 020 7620 2077
www.paxman.co.uk

Rose Morris
11 Denmark Street, WC2H 8LS
Tel: 020 7836 0991
www.rose-morris.co.uk

Jaques Samuel Pianos
142 Edgware Road, W2 2DZ
Tel: 020 7723 8818
www.jspianos.com

Magic

Davenports
Units 19-20 Charing Cross Con-
course, 5 Adelaide Street,
WC2N 4HZ
Tel: 020 7836 0408
www.davenportsmagic.co.uk

Publishers & Licence Holders

Music Sales
14-15 Berners Street, W1T 3LJ
Tel: 020 7612 7400
www.musicsales.com

Musicscope
95 White Lion Street, N1 9PF
Tel: 020 7278 1133

Warner Chappell Music
Griffin House, 161 Hammersmith
Road, W6 8BS
Tel: 020 8563 5800

Josef Weinberger
12 Mortimer Street, W1N 7RB
Tel: 020 7580 2827
www.josef-weinberger.co.uk

Education

Dance Schools

Central School of Ballet
10 Herbal Hill, Clerkenwell Road, EC1R 5EG
Tel: 020 7837 6332
www.centralschoolofballet.co.uk

Laban
Creekside, Deptford, SE8 3DZ
Tel: 020 8691 8600
www.laban.org

London Contemporary Dance School
The Place,
17 Duke's Road, WC1H 9PY
Tel: 020 7121 1111
www.theplace.org.uk

London Studio Centre
42-50 York Way, N1 9AB
Tel: 020 7837 7741
www.london-studio-centre.co.uk

Royal Academy of Dance
36 Battersea Square, SW11 3RA
Tel: 020 7326 8000
www.rad.org.uk

Royal Ballet School
46 Floral Street, WC2E 9DA
Tel: 020 7836 8899
www.royal-ballet-school.org.uk

Urdang Academy
Finsbury Town Hall, Rosebery Avenue, EC1R 4RP
Tel: 020 7836 5709
www.theurdangacademy.com

Drama Schools

Academy of Live & Recorded Arts
The Royal Victoria Patriotic Building, Fitzhugh Grove, Trinity Road, SW18 3SX
Tel: 020 8870 6475
www.alra.demon.co.uk

Arts Educational Schools
14 Bath Road, W4 1LY
Tel: 020 8987 6666
www.artsed.co.uk

Central School of Speech & Drama
Embassy Theatre, Eton Avenue, NW3 3HY
Tel: 020 7722 8183
www.cssd.ac.uk
In addition to full time training offers evening, weekend, summer and short courses.

Drama Centre London
Central Saint Martins College of Art & Design, 10 Back Hill, EC1R 5LQ
Tel: 020 7514 8778
www.csm.arts.ac.uk/drama/

Guildhall School of Music & Drama
Silk Street, EC2Y 8DT
Tel: 020 7628 2571
www.gsmd.ac.uk

**Italia Conti Academy
Of Theatre Arts**
*Avondale, 72 Landor Road,
SW9 9PH*
Tel: 020 7733 3210
www.italiaconti-acting.co.uk

**LAMDA - London Academy of
Music and Dramatic Art**
155 Talgarth Road, W14 9DA
Tel: 020 8834 0500
www.lamda.org.uk

**Mountview Academy
of Theatre Arts**
*Ralph Richardson Memorial Studios,
Clarendon Rd, Wood Green, N22 6XF*
Tel: 020 8881 2201
www.mountview.ac.uk

RADA - Royal Academy of Dramatic Art
62-64 Gower Street, WC1E 6ED
Tel: 020 7636 7076
www.rada.org
In addition to full time training offers evening, weekend, summer and short courses.

**Webber Douglas Academy of
Dramatic Art**
30 Clareville Street, SW7 5AP
Tel: 020 7370 4154
www.webberdouglasacademy.co.uk

Music Schools

Royal Academy of Music
Marylebone Road, NW1 5HT
Tel: 020 7873 7373
www.ram.ac.uk

Royal College of Music
Prince Consort Road, SW7 2BS
Tel: 020 7589 3643
www.rcm.ac.uk

Trinity College of Music
King Charles Court, Old Royal College, Greenwich, SE10 9JF
Tel: 020 8305 4444
www.tcm.ac.uk

Classes & Courses

The Actors Centre
1A Tower Street, WC2H 9NP
Tel: 020 7240 3940
www.actorscentre.co.uk

Circus Space
Coronet Street, N1 6HD
Tel: 020 7613 4141
www.thecircusspace.com

The City Lit
*Keeley Street (off Drury Lane),
WC2B 4BA*
Tel: 020 7492 2600
*Enrolment and information line:
020 7831 7831*
www.citylit.ac.uk

Goldsmiths College
Lewisham Way, SE14 6NW
Tel: 020 7919 7171
www.goldsmiths.ac.uk

Morley College
61 Westminster Bridge Road,
SE1 7HT
Tel: 020 7928 8501
www.morleycollege.ac.uk

Shakespeare's Globe Education
Programme
21 New Globe Walk, SE1 9DT
Tel: 020 7902 1433
www.shakespeares-globe.org
Staged Readings, lectures, courses
and workshops

Dance Studios

Dance Works
16 Balderton Street, W1V 1TF
Tel: 020 7629 6183
www.danceworks.co.uk

Pineapple Dance Centre
7 Langley Street, WC2H 9JA
Tel: 020 7836 4004
www.pineapple.uk.com

Contacts

Organisations

Arts Council of England
14 Great Peter Street, SW1P 3NQ
Tel: 0845 300 6200
www.artscouncil.org.uk

Artsline
54 Charlton Street, NW1 1HS
Tel: 020 7388 2227
www.artsline.org.uk

British Music Hall Society
Thurston Lodge, Thurston Park,
Whitstable, Kent, CT5 1RE
Tel/Fax: 01227 275959
www.music-hall-society.com

The British Puppet & Model Theatre Guild
65 Kingsley Ave, Ealing, W13 OEH
Tel: 020 89978236
www.puppetguild.org.uk

Department for Culture, Media & Sport
2 Cockspur Street, SW1Y 5DH
Tel:020 7211 6000
www.heritage.gov.uk

Equity - The British Actors Union Guild House
Upper St Martin's Lane, WC2H 9EG
Tel: 020 7379 6000
www.equity.org.uk

Frank Matcham Society
42 Ecclesbourne Drive, Buxton,
Derbyshire, SK17 9BW
Tel: 01298 26656
www.frankmatchamsociety.org.uk

Fringe Theatre Network
Old Red Lion Theatre,
418 St John Street, EC1V 4QE
Tel: 020 7833 3053
www.fringetheatre.org.uk

Haymarket Masterclasses
Theatre Royal Haymarket,
SW1Y 4HT
Tel: 020 7389 9660
www.masterclass.org.uk

The Irving Society
10 Kings Avenue, W5 2SH
Tel: 020 8566 8301
www.theirvingsociety.org.uk

The Mousetrap Foundation
Bedford Chambers, The Piazza,
Covent Garden, WC2E 8HA
Tel: 020 7836 4388
www.mousetrap.org.uk

Musician's Union
60-64 Clapham Road, SW9 0JJ
Tel: 020 7582 5566
www.musiciansunion.org.uk

National Campaign For The Arts
1 Kingly Street, W1B 5PA
Tel: 020 7287 3777
www.artscampaign.org.uk

National Council for Drama Training
1-7 Woburn Walk, WC1H 0JJ
Tel: 020 7387 3650
www.ncdt.co.uk

National Disability Arts Forum
59 Lime Street, Ouseburn Valley,
Newcastle upon Tyne, NE1 2PQ
Tel: 0191 261 1628
www.ndaf.org

Radar
Unit 12 City Forum, 250 City Road,
EC1V 8AF
Tel: 020 7250 3222
www.radar.org.uk

Save London's Theatres Campaign
Guild House, Upper St Martin's
Lane, WC2H 9EG
Tel: 020 7670 0270
www.savelondonstheatres.org.uk

Shape Ticket Scheme
London Voluntary Sector Resource
Centre, 356 Holloway Road, N7 6PA
Tel: 020 7619 6160
www.shapearts.org.uk

ShowPairs
Available to companies only (not
individuals) in London and the
home counties.
PO Box 3841, London, SW1V 2XE
Information line: 020 7976 5887
www.show-pairs.co.uk

ShowSavers
COBO Media,
43A Garthorne Road, SE23 1EP
Tel: 020 8291 7079
www.showsavers.com

SPIT - Signed Performances In
Theatre
6 Thirlmere Drive, Lymm
Cheshire, WA13 9PE
Tel: 01925 754 231
www.spit.org.uk

The Society For Theatre Research
1E Tavistock Street, WC2E 7PA
Tel: 020 7943 4700
www.str.org.uk

Society Of London Theatre
32 Rose Street, WC2E 9ET
Tel: 020 7557 6700
www.officiallondontheatre.co.uk

Stage One
32 Rose Street, WC2E 9ET
Tel: 020 7557 6737
www.stageone.uk.com

STAR - Society of Ticket Agents
and Retailers
PO Box 43, WC2H 7LD
Tel: 0870 603 9011
www.s-t-a-r.org.uk

Stagetext
First Floor, 54 Commercial Street,
E1 6LT
Tel: 020 7377 0540
www.stagetext.co.uk

The Theatres Trust
22 Charing Cross Road, WC2H 0HR
Tel: 020 7836 8591
www.theatrestrust.org.uk

Vocaleyes
First Floor, 54 Commercial Street,
E1 6LT
Tel: 020 7375 1043
www.vocaleyes.co.uk

Writers Guild Of Great Britain
15 Britannia Street, WC1X 9JN
Tel: 020 7833 0777
www.writersguild.org.uk

Producers

Act Productions
20-22 Stukeley Street, WC2B 5LR
Tel: 020 7438 9500

Michael Codron
Aldwych Theatre Offices, Aldwych, WC2B 4DF
Tel: 020 7240 8291

Robert Fox
6 Beauchamp Place, SW3 1NG
Tel: 020 7584 6855

Sonia Friedman
New Ambassadors Theatre, West Street, WC2H 9ND
Tel: 020 7395 5454

Bill Kenwright
106 Harrow Road, Off Howley Place, W2 1RR
Tel: 020 7446 6200
www.kenwright.com

Andrew Lloyd Webber (Really Useful Group)
22 Tower Street, W1V 5FD
Tel: 020 7240 0880
www.reallyuseful.com

Cameron Mackintosh
1 Bedford Square, WC1B 3RA
Tel: 020 7637 8866

Duncan Weldon
Suite 4, Waldorf Chambers, 11 Aldwych, WC2B 4DA
Tel: 020 7836 0186

Lyric Theatre, Door Detail

Bibliography

The Great Theatres Of London, *Ronald Bergan*
Prion, London, 1990

Britain In Old Photographs: Theatrical London, *Patricia Dee Berry*
Alan Sutton Publishing, Stroud, 1995

The Guinness Book of Theatre Facts & Feats, *Michael Billington*
Guinness Superlatives, London, 1982

The British Theatre, *Alec Clunes*
Cassell, London, 1964

The Theatres Trust Guide To British Theatres 1750-1950
John Earle & Michael Sell, A&C Black, London, 2000

The Streets Of London - A dictionary of the names and their origins
Sheila Fairfield, Macmillan, London, 1983

Victorian & Edwardian Theatres, *Victor Glassstone*
Thames & Hudson, London, 1975

Rebuilding Shakespeare's Globe, *Andrew Gurr & Ornell*
Weidenfeld & Nicolson, London, 1989

London Theatres And Music Halls 1850-1950, *Diana Howard*
Library Association, London, 1970

Theatre And Playhouse, *Richard and Helen Leacroft*
Methuen, London, 1984

The Lost Theatres Of London, *Raymond Mander & Joe Mitchenson*
Rupert Hart-Davis, London, 1968

The Theatres Of London, *Raymond Mander & Joe Mitchenson*
New English Library, London, 1975

Empires, Hippodromes & Palaces, *Jack Read*
The Alderman Press, London, 1985

London Theatre From The Globe To The National, *James Roose-Evans*
Phaidon, Oxford, 1977

Frank Matcham - Theatre Architect, *Brian Walker*
Blackstaff Press, Belfast, 1980

The Oberon Glossary Of Theatrical Terms (Theatre Jargon Explained)
Colin Winslow, Oberon Books, London, 1991

London Theatre Walks, *Jim D Young & John Miller*
Applause, New York, 1998

Photography Credits

All images but the ones listed below are photographed by Derek Kendall © English Heritage.

p.89 Royal National Theatre © Gautier Deblonde / p106-107 Open Air, Regents Park © Alastair Muir / p.129 Royal Opera House © Rob Moore / p. 141 Shakespeare's Globe © Donald Cooper /p.166 The Royal Opera House © Rob Moore/ p.178 Sarastro © Natalie Pecht.

Theatre Index

Index

General Index

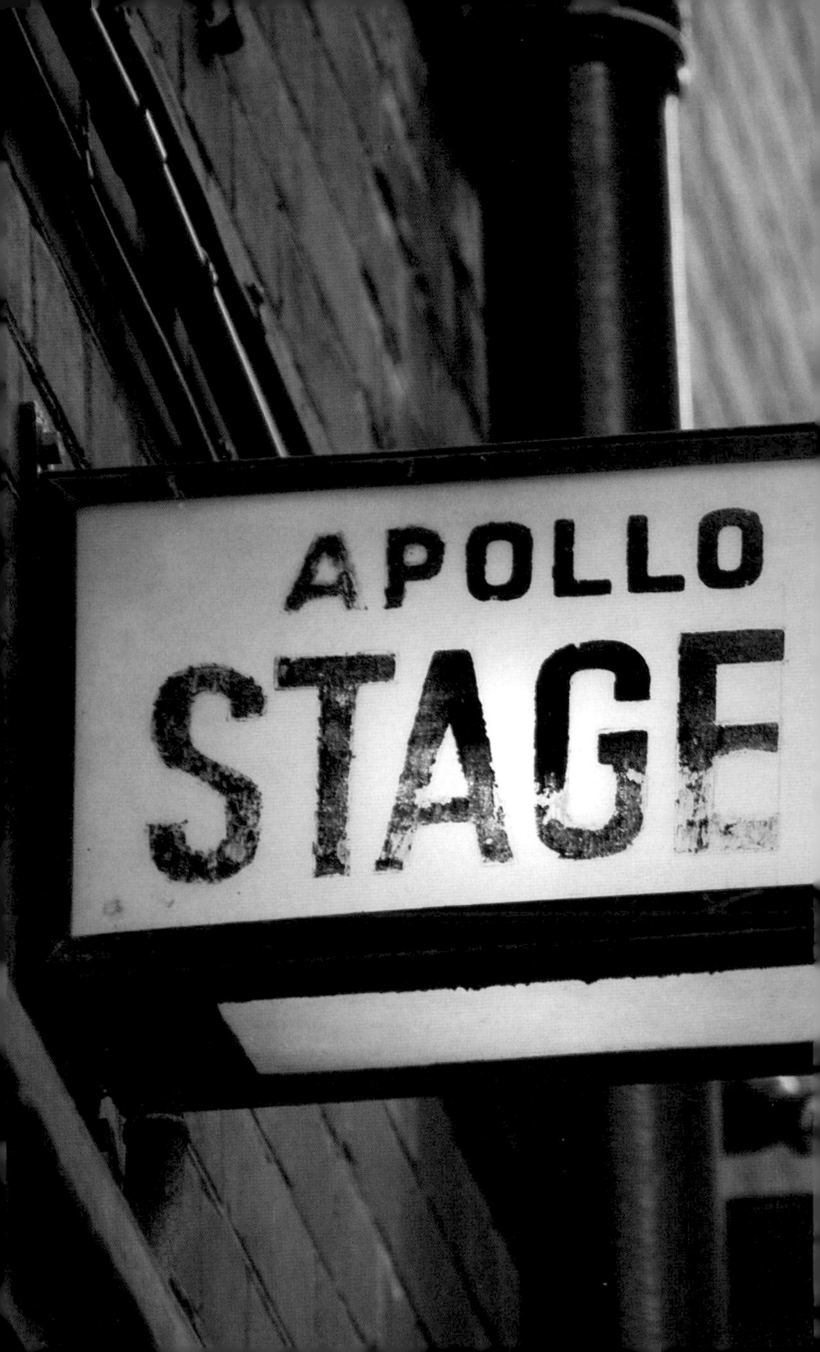
APOLLO
STAGE

HEATRE
DOOR

Order our other Metro Titles

The following titles are also available from Metro Publications. Please send your order along with a cheque made payable to Metro Publications to the address below. Postage and packaging free.

Alternatively call our customer order line on 020 8533 7777 (Visa/Mastercard/Switch), Open Mon-Fri 9am-6pm

Metro Publications
PO Box 6336, London N1 6PY
info@metropublications.com
www.metropublications.com

London Market Guide
Andrew Kershman
£6.99 ISBN 1-902910-14-1

Bargain Hunters' London
Andrew Kershman
£6.99 ISBN 9781902910277

Food Lovers' London
Jenny Linford
£8.99 ISBN 1-902910-22-2